Designing the
Natural Landscape

Designing the Natural Landscape

By

Richard L. Austin, ASLA

VNR VAN NOSTRAND REINHOLD COMPANY
NEW YORK CINCINNATI TORONTO LONDON MELBOURNE

Copyright © 1984 by Van Nostrand Reinhold Company Inc.

Library of Congress Catalog Card Number: 82-23751
ISBN: 0-442-20978-9

Manufactured in the United States of America

Published by Van Nostrand Reinhold Company Inc.
135 West 50th Street
New York, N.Y. 10020

Van Nostrand Reinhold Company Limited
Molly Millars Lane
Wokingham, Berkshire, England

Van Nostrand Reinhold
480 Latrobe Street
Melbourne, Victoria 3000, Australia

Macmillan of Canada
Division of Gage Publishing Limited
164 Commander Boulevard
Agincourt, Ontario M1S 3C7, Canada

15 14 13 12 11 10 9 8 7 6 5 4 3 2 1

Library of Congress Cataloging in Publication Data

Austin, Richard L.
    Designing the natural landscape.

    Includes index.
    1. Landscape architecture.   2. Landscape gardening.
I. Title.
SB472.A867 1983   712   82-23751
ISBN 0-442-20978-9

INTRODUCTION

As designers, we often consider ourselves the creators of the environments in which we live. We manipulate spaces to withstand the horizontal and vertical pressures of human compaction and term the endeavor urban living. When horizontal and vertical limits are exhausted, we simply restructure the contours and alter the drainage patterns to better suit what we feel is the natural order of priorities.

Only within the last few decades have we begun to overlay our needs onto the natural environments. We no longer arbitrarily label the forces of nature destructive, but study the inevitable consequences of alteration when we design. We know now to venture to the far reaches of the natural order and learn from the existing elements before leaning upon them with our design efforts.

As technological hardware converts us to multiples of unseen statistics, we return to the "natural order" for advice and consent before creating. We sometimes overlook the importance of the natural vegetation that covers our planet, however. The trees that shade the soil, the shrubs that feed the wildlife, and the grasses that prevent erosion are all links in a very important chain of environmental events.

This text is a basic guide for the architect, the engineer, the landscape architect, and the planner for developing—or redeveloping—an arrangement of plant materials that follow their originally intended directive. Use it as it is intended to be used—as a tool for design. Regardless of the ecological forces that exist on our world, we are still designers. Let's just do it naturally.

NATURAL VS. NATIVE

It is important at this initial stage of the text to identify the differences between the natural and the native landscapes. Although to some designers these terms are almost synonymous, the specific association of the expressions to a developed project lies in the final application of plant materials.

The *natural* landscape is comprised of ecologically placed species of plant materials and is void of any formal human manipulation in the selection, location, or perpetuation of the vegetative compositions. The processes that create or fulfill the biological needs of an environment must be those that have been within nature for eons of time. Any duplication of those processes in order to regenerate a specific set of ecological conditions in a composition is not a "natural" landscape. It is, however, a "naturalistic" arrangement which attempts to reestablish a set of conditions favorable to the growth and development of ecologically selected plant materials.

The *native* landscape, on the other hand, is a planting

composition with introduced materials originally from another geographic or ecological locale that have been transferred into their new setting for a specific, ornamental purpose. The grass, shrub, or tree species may be readily adaptable to the new environment, but it is not a "natural" process that has placed them in their new community.

THE CONSTRAINTS OF THE NATURAL DESIGN

Many designers feel the development of a landscape composition following the natural processes of the plant systems offers a greater flexibility for creativity than does a project based more on traditional ornamental requirements. On the contrary, the natural, or naturalistic, setting demands more preplanning research, analysis efforts, and problem-solving tasks than does any other approach to a landscape problem. Local development regulations that will often control the final determination are more numerous and less flexible than those from higher governmental authorities. Local political climates often favor a more expeditious solution for the promotion of campaign promises. Short-term economic gains or reduced investment capabilities may overshadow the needed ecological rejuvenation of a given site. There are, in fact, more unforeseeable obstacles in the path of the designer from this type of effort than in the more traditional projects. To assist in removing these blocks to design creativity, extensive research should be directed into the following areas.

1. *Laws and regulations.* On the national level, the Endangered Species Act may control the collection of seeds or the propagation of plants on the endangered list. Local, state, or even regional restrictions may prohibit the use of certain species because they are alternate hosts of diseases or may become noxious weeds in certain situations. Either the original host or the alternate host may be prohibited. Many municipal governments may restrict the height of grasses used as a lawn or groundcover mass. Most state agricultural departments or agents of the U.S. Soil Conservation Service can supply information on prohibited materials.

2. *Aesthetic considerations.* The choice of plant materials may determine whether the composition is a naturalized arrangement of ornamental materials or a naturalized arrangement of locally collected plants. A highly manicured setting may be out of place on a rural farmstead, and a naturalized arrangement of locally collected materials may be out of place in a controlled housing development.

3. *Management strategies.* To have a successful design composition, there must be a cohesive environment that meets the needs of both the plant material and the animal life that supports it. In managing the project after planting, chemical stimulants, growth retardants, or fertilizers may be important for proper growth and conditioning. Government agencies or public opinion at the local level may prohibit the use of these substances.

4. *Economic considerations.* One of the major goals of most landscape projects is to develop as much area of the site as possible with the minimum amount of investment. Costs can be raised or lowered by the following:

   a. The use of mechanical irrigation systems
   b. Complicated planting techniques
   c. The spacing of the plant materials
   d. Mechanical support for severe slope stabilization
   e. The size of the planted materials (smaller plants often survive the initial planting "shock

period" because of a more favorable root:top ratio)

5. *Time considerations.* Since it is difficult to drive to the local garden center and buy the needed plant materials, time must be budgeted to grow or collect the desired items. Some species must be dormant for specific periods of time before germination is attempted. Topsoil may need to be in place days or even months before formal planting operations begin. If a "natural planting" process is the intent of the project, both the client and the designer must be prepared to invest a great amount of time to reach their objectives.

Based upon our previous definitions, it is essentially impossible for a designer to create a *natural* landscape composition. The hundreds of years that are needed to reach a climax stage of plant growth will overrule any simple human endeavor. Therefore, as a matter of basic semantics, we will apply our terms to the specific *intent* of the design project. If the goal is to create a naturalized setting of locally collected plant species and arrange them based upon their original habitation, the resulting composition will be called a *natural landscape.* If ornamental materials are to be selected and planted in a non-formal arrangement, the composition will be called a *native landscape.*

Whether to fashion a congenial living environment or to perpetuate the harmonious balance between predator and prey, the *natural landscape* may well be the one design alternative that will release the inevitable pressures upon the remaining ecological systems. With the *natural landscape,* we may be able to rebuild those values that have been lost through years of over-decoration.

NOTE: The terms *natural* and *native* are used in this context based upon the intent and the process that places the plant materials upon the site. Native plant species are in most instances used as ornamental fillers and are not properly applied to the natural landscape.

ACKNOWLEDGMENTS

I wish to express my appreciation to the U.S. Department of Agriculture, Soil Conservation Service, Lincoln, Nebraska, for allowing me to spend an extensive amount of time investigating their records and library for information on the development of the natural landscape. I am also indebted to the firms of Johnson, Johnson, and Roy, Inc. and to LeRoy Troyer and Associates for allowing me to use excerpts from several of their natural landscape projects. Their works appear as case studies in Appendix 5.

CONTENTS

1. THE NATURAL SYSTEMS

THE PLANT COMMUNITIES IN THE NATURAL LANDSCAPE

Because of the complexities of the natural landscape, it is important for a designer to fully understand the communities of plant materials that may exist on any proposed project site. Any preplanning effort that involves the analysis and inventory of a resource base should be first supplemented by an investigation of plant ecological regions. Only with this broader understanding will it be possible to gain an adequate interpretation of the local plant communities.

The dynamic relationship between the various vegetative systems found on a project site, or those that might be introduced in the design, are governed by a number of ecological factors: climate, physiography, and soil. In order to focus specific attention upon the individual species used in the project, a careful review of these ecological factors is important. For it is these factors, more than anything else, that will determine the geographic range and possible design functions of a natural vegetative community.

The *climate* of the plant community includes the temperature, precipitation, humidity, light, and wind that act in unison from day to day and season to season to comprise its major design characteristic. *Temperature,* one of the most important characteristics, will cause one plant type to thrive and reproduce while depriving another of the essential components for life (Fig. 1-1).

Precipitation is the amount of moisture that falls on the community during a specified period of time. It is usually gauged in inches and hundredths of inches and will largely control the distribution of the vegetation. Where the rainfall is heavy, a climax community could easily be a dense forest. Where it is not, a community can sustain only desertlike growth and will never reach its climax stage (Fig. 1-2).

The amount of water vapor in the air represents *humidity,* with relative humidity corresponding to the percentage of air saturation. Air can hold more water vapor when the temperature rises; thus when air is heated, relative humidity is lowered, and vise versa. When plants cool at night and the adjacent air reaches a relative humidity of 100 percent, excess moisture results and falls to the ground in the form of dew or frost—depending on the temperature. (Dice, 1952; Shelford, 1963; and Watt, 1968)

Photosynthesis, via solar radiation, is the basis for the existence of every plant community. It is this *light* that provides the essential ingredient for the production of food for the plants, which in turn controls the geographic range of the community.

Wind plays an important role in the natural community

1

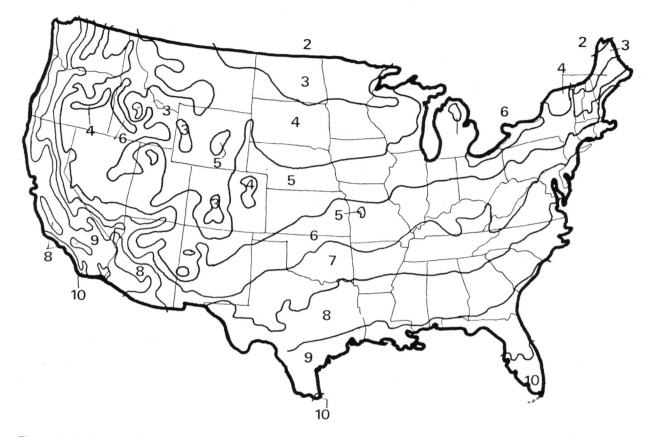

Figure 1–1. Average Annual Minimum Temperature Zones

Zone	Temperature Range
3	−40 to −30
4	−30 to −20
5	−20 to −10
6	−10 to 0
7	0 to 10
8	10 to 20
9	20 to 30
10	30 to 40

Figure 1-2. Figure 1-2. Average Annual Precipitation (inches) for North America. (From USDA, *Yearbook of Agriculture,* 1963, p. 100)

by aiding in the dispersal of pollen, seeds, or insects that are vital for the continuation of basic community characteristics. High winds, or sudden wind changes, may cause damage to some plant species or even reduce the amount of water vapor in the air. In some vegetative communities, the direction of growth and even the shape of some plants will be controlled by winds.

The basic *physiography* of a plant community, the second ecological factor, can be determined by looking at a region's geologic history. The degree of slope of a project site will govern the amount of light it receives for plant growth. On level areas where the grade is fairly uniform, the transition of plants may be very broad and indefinite. On mountains and steep slopes, near saline areas, or around water, there may be a very small and defined plant community. (Shelford, 1963; Spurr and Barnes, 1964)

The solid material covering the surface of the community habitat is called *soil,* the third ecological factor. It is the major supporter of plant development and its character is the most important factor in natural vegetation. A soil will govern the topography of the community, the rate of water runoff, the amount of root moisture, and the ability of the community to reach a climax stage. The more unstable soil bases (sandy soils) will not allow proper root development for the larger climax plants, which result in less progressive vegetative communities.

On a *micro* scale, the local environmental conditions of the site must be determined by careful resource inventory. For a *macro* scale determination, however, the vegetative regions discussed below are presented for preplanning assistance.

The United States is made up of 32 general growth regions, which stretch from the North Pacific Coast to the southern tip of Florida (Fig. 1-3). These regions, in turn, may be divided into various forest and grassland communities.

The North American Deciduous Forest

This forest community occupies North America from the Gulf of Mexico to the Great Lakes (Fig. 1-4). It is found on the northern Florida Peninsula westward beyond the Mississippi River and is dominated by trees with broad leaves that shed each season. Small deciduous trees and shrubs occupy its understory. The beech or sugar maple will comprise the climax stand of this area. (Shelford, 1963; Spurr and Barnes, 1964)

The subdivisions of this forest are: the northern and upland region (Fig. 1-5); the southern and lowland region (Fig. 1-6); and the stream-skirting forest. The natural landscape is characterized by mixed plant materials and a lack of a distinctive boundary between regions. The northern and upland region has five subregional areas, which are comprised of the following vegetative types (Shelford, 1963):

1. *Tulip-oak.* This part of the forest is most abundant between altitudes of 500 feet (150 m) and 1,000 feet (300 m).
2. *Oak-chestnut.* This area is found from Cape Ann, Massachusetts, to the southern end of the Appalachians at the higher elevations.
3. *Maple-basswood-birch.* This forest area is found primarily on the mountainsides in the Appalachians at altitudes of from 2,500 feet (760 m) to 4,200 feet (1,275 m).
4. *Maple-beech-hemlock.* These are found in southern Michigan, northern Ohio, and Indiana.
5. *Maple-basswood.* These are found in northern Illinois, southern Wisconsin, and parts of eastern Minnesota.

The mean annual rainfall of this forest area ranges from 28 inches (70 cm) to 40 inches (100 cm). The trees of

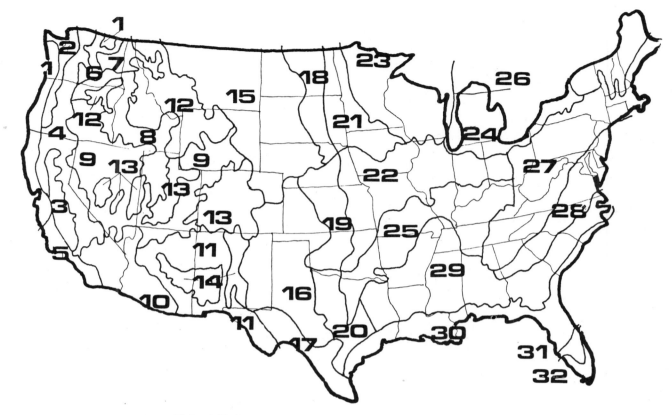

Figure 1-3.   Plant Growth Regions of the United States

1 North Pacific Coast	12 Northern Rocky Mountains	23 Western Great Lakes
2 Willamette Valley—Puget Sound	13 Central Rocky Mountains	24 Central Great Lakes
3 Central California Valleys	14 Southern Rocky Mountains	25 Ozark-Ohio-Tennessee River Valleys
4 Cascade Sierra Nevada	15 Northern Great Plains	26 Northern Great Lakes—St. Lawrence
5 Southern California	16 Central Great Plains	27 Appalachian
6 Columbia River Valley	17 Southern Plains	28 Piedmont
7 Palouse-Bitteroot Valley	18 Northern Black Soils	29 Upper Coastal Plain
8 Snake River Plain—Utah Valley	19 Central Black Soils	30 Swampy Coastal Plain
9 Great Basin-Intermontane	20 Southern Black Soils	31 South-Central Florida
10 Southwestern Desert	21 Northern Prairies	32 Subtropical Florida
11 Southern Plateau	22 Central Prairies	

(From "Landscapes for Living," *USDA Yearbook,* 1972, p. 1)

the forest canopy are 75 feet (23 m) to 100 feet (30 m) in height and 23 inches (58 cm) to 30 inches (76 cm) in caliper. Their branching heights are 32 feet (10 m) to 40 feet (12 m), and they shade about 90 percent of the forest floor. (Shelford, 1963)

The *canopy layer* is made up of the limbs, upper trunk, and leaves of the dominant forest vegetation. The *understory* is comprised of young and suppressed individuals of the larger species, while the *seedling trees* (or larger shrubs) are the abundant pawpaw. The spicebush is the dominant material of the *shrub* layers, and the *herb* layer is characterized by common nettle and wild ginger. (Dice, 1952; Shelford, 1963)

The southern and lowland forests are subdivided into:

1. *Oak-hickory.* These are found primarily from New Jersey to Alabama and westward to Texas.
2. *Magnolia-maritime.* This begins in the corner of Virginia, extends southward to meet the magnolia forest in South Carolina, and goes along the coast to the southeast corner of Texas.

Rainfall for this region is from 40 inches (100 cm) to 60 inches (150 cm) annually and is greatest in the spring and summer. (Shelford, 1963; Spurr and Barnes, 1964)

The Floodplain Forest

These communities are mixed with deciduous forests and grassland areas of North America (Fig. 1-7). Due to constantly changing environmental conditions brought on by shifting channels, islands, and sandbars, the vegetation often stops short of reaching the climax stage.

Two types of natural landscape habitats are characteristic of this area. The first is *terrestial,* which is dry at low water, and the second is *aquatic,* which is covered with water most of the year. Early spring flooding that causes a submergence of vegetation from a week to as long as two months is typical of these forest areas. (Shelford, 1963)

Small tree thickets are common, especially the sandbar willow, which helps stabilize sands along river channels. These are usually followed immediately by cottonwood seedlings, and then by sugarberry, elm, and sweetgum. Several hundred years may be necessary for an oak forest to appear on areas 40 feet (12 m) to 45 feet (14 m) above the low water level. (Dice, 1952; and Shelford, 1963)

The Boreal Coniferous Forest

This forest originally extended from some parts of Indiana and Ohio, to the Mackenzie River in Canada, to the Brooks Mountain Range in Alaska. (Fig. 1-8). The climate ranges from cool to cold, and there is precipitation all year, with much coming in the summer. The climax evergreens may be the pines with long needles, or the spruce, hemlock, and fir with short, thick leaves.

This forest area can be subdivided into the boreal forest east of the Rocky Mountains into Newfoundland; the vegetation of the valley areas and lower slopes of the northern Rocky Mountains; and the forests of the Rocky Mountains and the Sierra Nevadas. (Shelford, 1963)

The Montane Coniferous Forest and Alpine Communities

This region is found from the upper eastern slope of the British Columbia coastal mountains, the Cascade Mountains, and the coast range of northern California. Its eastern boundary is the Boreal Forest of the north and the Great Plains grassland (Fig. 1-9). Alpine meadows occur at higher elevations above this forest's vegetation, while various woodlands occur below at lower elevations. (Shelford, 1963; Watt, 1968)

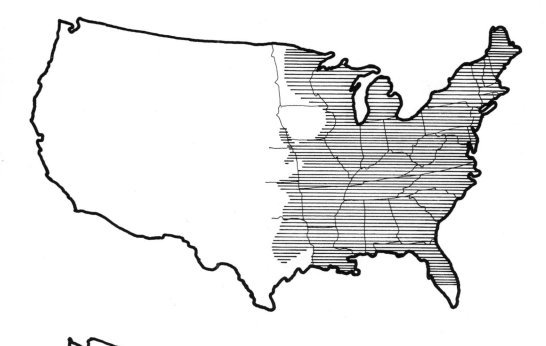

Figure 1-4. This North American Deciduous Forest is dominated by trees with broad leaves that shed each season.

Figure 1-5. This Northern and Upland region is part of the North American Deciduous Forest and is comprised of large, overstory vegetation.

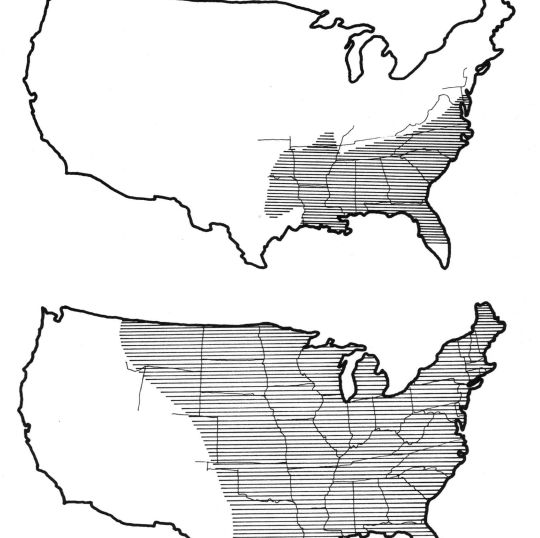

Figure 1-6. This Southern and Lowland region is part of the North American Deciduous Forest and is comprised mainly of the Oak-Hickory-Magnolia forests.

Figure 1-7. This Floodplain Forest area is characterized by the terrestial (low water) and equatic (covered with water) vegetative types.

8

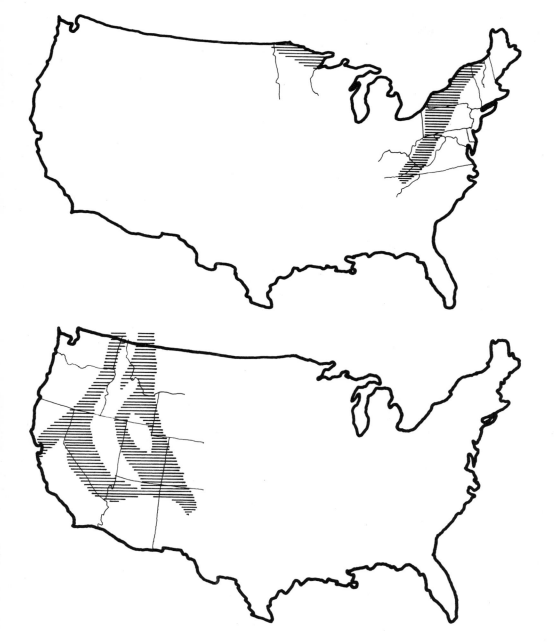

Figure 1–8. This Boreal Coniferous Forest is divided into the boreal forest east of the Rocky Mountains, and the vegetation of the valley areas of the northern Rocky Mountains.

Figure 1–9. This Montane Coniferous Forest and Alpine communities is characterized by alpine meadows, and woodland areas at lower elevations.

9

The Northern Pacific Coast-Rainy Western Hemlock Forest

This forest area is found adjacent to the Pacific Coast from the middle of California to southern Alaska (Fig. 1-10). The mature, dominant vegetation is very tall—125 feet (38 m) to 300 feet (90 m)—and up to 20 feet (6 m) wide. Understory trees or shrubs may find it impossible to survive unless openings are provided in the canopy. (Shelford, 1963; Watt, 1968)

Shrub and herb layers cannot develop properly in the mature forest and are restricted to a few species. The frost-free period will vary from 120 days to 210 days, with a mean annual temperature range from 40° F (4° C) to 56° F (13° C).

The Broad Sclerophyll-Grizzly Bear Community

This vegetation ranges from central Oregon through California and may be either forest, woodland, or chaparral (Fig. 1-11). Fewer than 20 percent of the dominant species are deciduous.

Annual rainfall in the northern end ranges from 16 inches (40 cm) to 38 inches (95 cm), and in the southern chaparral vegetation averages 21.6 inches (54 cm) when not in the June through September rainless season. (Dice, 1952; Shelford, 1963; and Watt, 1968)

The sclerophyll vegetation will vary from a large oak forest with a grass ground cover, to a scattered woodland of trees with a chaparral or sagebrush undergrowth, to a bush vegetation. (Dice, 1952; and Shelford, 1963)

The Desert and Semidesert Communities

These communities occupy the Great Basin portion of western Utah and the largest part of Nevada, and extend into Death Valley of California (Fig. 1-12). The vegetation is shrubby and is dominated by sagebrush, with some contact with ponderosa pine forests.

Rainfall for most of this area will average below 10 inches. The temperature in January will average between 29° F (−1.7° C) and 39° F (3.9° C), with July averaging between 70° F (21° C) and 78° F (26° C). The major plants are deciduous shrubs and dense stands of tall sagebrush. (Dice, 1952; Shelford, 1963)

The Woodland and Brushland Communities

This vegetation occurs in the foothills from Montana and Oregon to Mexico (Fig. 1-13). It is characterized by short-trunked trees, a scattered growth of shrubs and herbs, and a dense growth of shrubs thinning into grassland and desert at lower elevations. The annual rainfall is from 12 inches (30 cm) to 25 inches (62 cm), and the temperature of the seasons is quite variable.

The following specific communities may be recognized: the western juniper-buckbrush region; the pinyon-juniper region; the oak-juniper region; the oak woodland region; and the oak bushland. (Shelford, 1963; Watt, 1968)

The Northern Grasslands

This vegetative region is characterized by perennial grasses stretching from Alberta to Mexico City, and the Pacific Coast to western Indiana (Fig. 1-14). The northern part is moist and cool; the southern part is drier. There are four major grassland areas important in this natural landscape. (Shelford, 1963; Watt, 1968)

The Tall-grass Prairie

This grass range once extended through what is now the Midwest agricultural region of the United States, from Manitoba to Oklahoma and eastward into Ohio and southern Michigan. It is now extensively plowed and is principally found in Kansas, the northern parts of Oklahoma,

Nebraska, and North and South Dakota. The major species of grasses are the bluestems (*Andropogon spp.*), porcupinegrass (*Stipa spp.*), switchgrass (*Panicum spp.*), Indiangrass (*Sorghastrum spp.*), and wild rye (*Elymus spp.*). The average height of these grasses is 4 to 5 feet (1 to 2 m) with a root depth reaching to 8 feet (2 m). The coastal prairie occupies the southern extension of this growth region inland from the coastal marshes of Texas and Louisiana. (Shelford, 1963; Watt, 1968)

The Mixed-grass Prairie

This grass region occupies the area between the tall-grass prairie and the foothills of the Rocky Mountains, extending from Canada to Texas, and expands westward from Texas to Arizona. It is often referred to as the short-grass prairie, but has intermediate-height grass species.

The major type of species include the western wheatgrass (*Agropyron smithii spp.*), needle-and-thread (*Stipa comata spp.*), green needlegrass (*S. viridula spp.*), prairie Junegrass (*Koeleria spp.*), blue grama grass (*Bouteloua gracilis spp.*), and buffalo grass (*Buchloe dactyloides spp.*). (Shelford, 1963; Watt, 1968)

The Semidesert Grassland

This area extends from central and southwestern Texas to northern Arizona and is the driest of the grassland regions. The species within this group have a short, open growth characteristic and are dominated by black gramma (*Bouteloua eriopoda spp.*), three-awn grasses (*Aristida spp.*), and curly mesquite (*Hilaria Belangeri* spp.). Tobosa grass (*Hilaria mutica spp.*) and alkali sacaton (*Sporobolus airoides spp.*) are characteristic to low sites that become flooded on occasion. (Shelford, 1963)

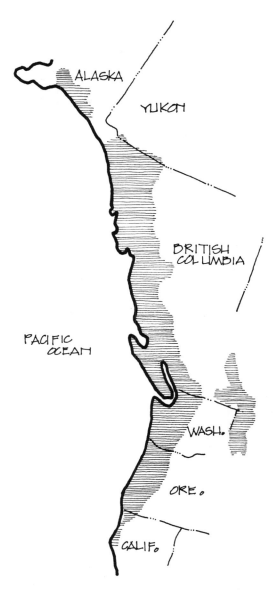

Figure 1-10. This Northern Pacific Coast-Rainy Western Hemlock Forest has dominant overstory reaching as high as 300 feet (91m) tall.

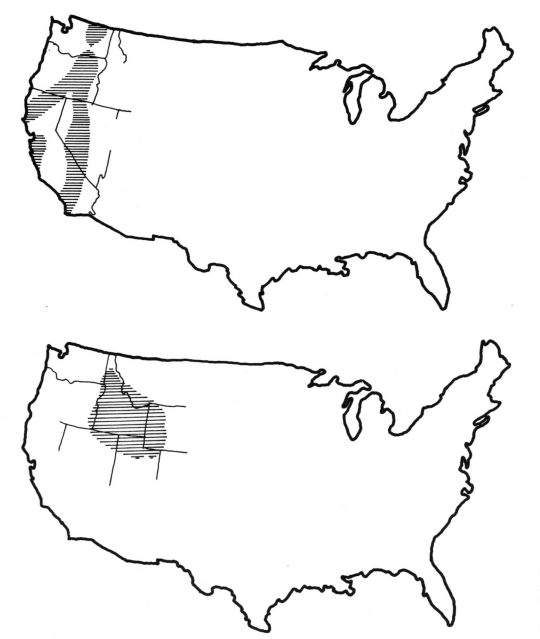

Figure 1–11. This Broad Schler-ophyll-Grizzly Bear community is dominated by evergreen vegetation, and has less than 20 percent deciduous plant material.

Figure 1–12. These Desert and Semidesert communities have few trees, and are dominated by deciduous shrubs and sagebrush.

Figure 1–13. These Woodland and Brushland communities are characterized by short-trunked trees, scattered shrubs, and grassland areas.

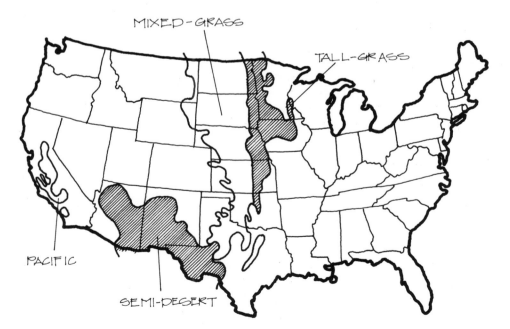

MIXED-GRASS

TALL-GRASS

PACIFIC

SEMI-DESERT

Figure 1–14. The Northern Grasslands are the Tall-grass Prairie, and Mixed-grass Prairie, the Semidesert grassland, and the Pacific Prairie.

The Pacific Prairie

This grassland prairie once covered an extensive portion of the valleys and foothills of California, northward into Oregon and Washington; into northern Utah and southern Idaho; south central Montana, southwestern Wyoming, northern Nevada; and western Alberta.

Important species of this region include wild oats (*Avena fatua spp.*), ripgut (*Bromus riqidus spp.*), purple needlegrass (*Stipa pulchra spp.*), wild ryes (*Elymus spp.*), Idaho fescue (*Festuca idahoensis spp.*), Sandbag bluegrass (*Poa secunda spp.*), and prairie Junegrass (*Koeleria spp.*). (Watt, 1968)

The Hot Desert

The vegetation of this community (Fig. 1-15) is adapted to conditions of small and irregularly occurring rainfalls, usually warm seasons, and very hot summers. It consists of mostly brush-covered areas, with a large portion of the surface exposed. The most dominant vegetation is creosote bush.

Western portions stretch from lower California into Arizona; the eastern part reaches from New Mexico into Texas. Dominant plants are small and rarely exceed 30 feet (9 m) in height; they are widely spaced due to low soil moisture. There is an extensive habitat diversity, with marked differences between slope orientation, sun exposure, and uplands versus lowlands.

The wide variation in habitats causes a complex vegetation distribution and a slow change in site characteristics from one plant type to another. Succession is, therefore, slow and difficult to distinguish. (Shelford, 1963; Watt, 1968)

Southern Florida

The vegetation of this area (Fig. 1-16) is varied and displays three probable climax stages: subtropical hammocks with a mixture of northern plant varieties; tropical hammocks; and dry and scrubby vegetation on the Keys. Rainfall occurs 12 months a year, with an occasional frost. The tropical and subtropical portions of the communities are below 23 feet (7 m) above sea level. (Shelford, 1963; Watt, 1968)

BASIC ECOLOGICAL PRINCIPLES

Designers have avoided the use of natural vegetation in a landscape composition for a number of reasons. A carryover attitude from the pioneer viewpoint has associated natural vegetation with hard work and something to be conquered. Some clients feel that the use of existing vegetation is the lazy way out, thus little attention and respect has been paid to its usage. The primary reason, however, is that most designers simply lack an adequate understanding of the processes that control natural vegetation.

In recent years, natural vegetation has become increasingly valued for landscape developments. It provides a greater choice of plant materials for use in the composition, often requires less maintenance, and is now more aesthetically appealing to both client and designer. Natural vegetation is either:

1. The community of native plants that develop within an area without manipulation by humans; or
2. A modification of the original plant community that retains most of its basic appearance and stability.

Factors Controlling the Ecosystems

The kind of natural ecosystem occurring in a particular place is a function of the climate, the parent substrate, the topography, the organisms present, and fire—all act-

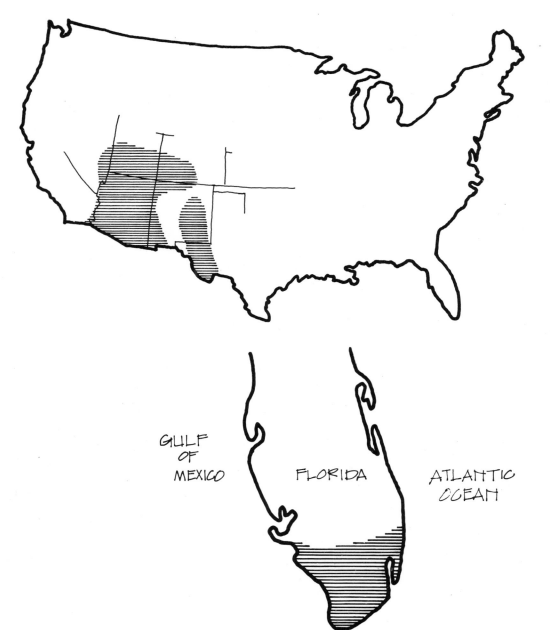

Figure 1-15. The vegetation of the Hot Desert is very adapted to small and irregularly occuring rainfalls.

GULF
OF
MEXICO

FLORIDA

ATLANTIC
OCEAN

Figure 1-16. The vegetation of Southern Florida is characterized by three probable climax stages: subtropical hammocks, tropical hammocks, and dry and scrubby vegetation.

ing through time. If even one of these influences is changed appreciably, the ecosystem is changed. Thus, due to differences in climates, there are broadleaf evergreen forest ecosystems in the moist tropics, deciduous forest ecosystems in moist temperate zones, and grassland and desert ecosystems in drier areas. Because of differences in soils, there are tall-grass ecosystems in sand and short-grass ecosystems in adjacent loam soils in the same semiarid climate. Due to topographic position, there are upland and lowland forest ecosystems. Some of these ecosystems are burned frequently by nature or human influence and, as a result, are different from unburned areas in the same region.

The variability among and within ecosystems complicates the basic understanding of these relationships. Besides the variability due to differences in climate, soil, topography, organisms, and fire, each ecosystem changes with time. An area whose potential is a beech-maple forest, for example, may be a thicket of shrubs because of a combination of past events, such as several frequent and severe fires; or a prairie may become a weed patch because of overgrazing. These changes over time are due to many causes, which can, with difficulty, be grouped into two categories.

First, some changes are due to outside or extraneous forces like tornadoes, hurricanes, and volcanic ash or lava deposits which destroy the prior vegetation. Second, other changes are due to intrinsic forces within the ecosystem, such as replacement of shortleaf pine by oak and hickory because the pines need an open area for the young to prosper, but young oak and hickory can grow under older trees. Fire is considered an extrinsic force at times and at other times, an intrinsic force, depending on its frequency, severity, and cause.

Ecologists have commonly used *ecological succession* for the replacement of one group of organisms by another due to intrinsic forces (Fig. 1-17). Annuals are the first plants that occur in fields abandoned from cultivation because they are adapted to rapid spread into bare, open areas. Within the first few years, perennials gradually invade, and when enough perennials get started to fully occupy the area, they eventually eliminate the annuals. With well-developed roots and a much larger food supply, these perennials can get water and nutrients more easily than seedlings can, and, therefore, they grow stronger and more dominant. Annuals must start as seedlings each year.

The white pine is often more successful in getting seeds into abandoned fields than are most other trees. It needs only an open area low in competition, and the abandoned field meets this requirement. However, as the pines develop into an old forest, the seeds, although more abundant than any other kind of tree, fail to produce new trees because the seedlings are not adapted to withstand the root competition and shading of older trees. On the other hand, the sugar maple, yellow birch, beech, and eastern hemlock can grow under the pines.

Over the decades, seeds of these more tolerant plants get into the pine forest and start a young hardwood stand. When the pines are removed by windthrow, disease, lumbering, or other causes, there is already a young forest of beech, birch, maple and hemlock that prevents the redevelopment of the pine. As the young hardwoods and hemlocks grow old, other kinds of trees cannot survive under them. They soon perpetuate themselves until a crown forest fire, clearing for agriculture, or some other severe disturbance opens up the space for pine reestablishment.

Typically, ecological successions end in a stable or selfperpetuating stage, provided outside disturbances are absent. This selfperpetuating stage is called the *climax stage.* Ecological successions, however, are not

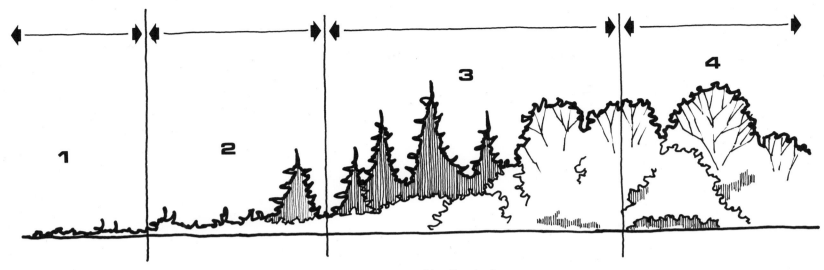

Figure 1-17. Secondary succession is the most commonly encountered by the designer.

Area #1: Annual weeds, 1–5 years for development
Area #2: Perennial grass, shrubs, and young white pine, 3–20 years for development
Area #3: Old White Pine with Young Hardwoods Underneath, 75–150 years for development
Area #4: Self-replacing birch-beech-maple forest, 200 + years for development

entirely predictable either in regard to composition or to rate of vegetative development. To understand fully, there are several things a designer should know:

1. The composition of the vegetation prior to the disturbance
2. The type of disturbance
3. The soil conditions and topography
4. The weather conditions, week by week and year by year, following the disturbance
5. The size of the disturbance
6. The composition of vegetation adjacent to the disturbed area
7. All the agents like fire and storms that occur during the successional process

Major Types of Vegetative Development

Successions have often been divided into primary and secondary. Primary successions start on areas that have not previously supported plants and animals; secondary successions start on areas that have a soil present.
Primary successions are divided into:

1. *Successions starting or relatively dry sites,* such as rock outcroppings. A characteristic sequence starts with lichens. Then, as crevices become filled with fine particles of weathered rock, mosses and herbs develop. Then a forest or grassland follows, depending on the climatic conditions. Such successions take from many hundreds to many thousands of

years before a continuous soil is produced from the rock outcroppings.

2. *Successions starting in ponds or lakes* left by such actions as glaciation. Over thousands of years, the pond becomes filled by the accumulation of dead plants. Algae and other submerged plants grow, die and settle to the bottom—not decomposing as quickly as they accumulate. As the bottom gets more shallow, emergent plants (bulrushes, sedges; and, finally, shrubs and trees) become established when the peat-soil builds up above the water level. In a few thousand years, 20, 30, or even 40 feet (6.1 m, 9.15 m or 12.2 m) of peat can accumulate in small lakes or ponds, allowing a forest to grow where the pond once occurred.

3. *Successions starting on ground-up rocks,* such as glacial till. Although ground-up rock is present in these areas, it is not a soil. It will not become soil until the rock particles chemically weather to free nutrients needed by plants and until there is an abundance of humus. These successions are much quicker than those starting in bedrock or ponds, but they are slower than secondary successions.

Secondary successions occur when a soil is still present after some disturbance that removes much or all of the existing plant cover (Fig. 1-17). Crown fire, lumbering, and abandonment of cultivation can result in the beginning of this type, provided the soil remains.

THE LIFE FORMS OF PLANTS

It is important to understand the forms that a plant will take in its natural habitat (Fig. 1-18). Nature has designed a unique relationship between plants and the environment, and this relationship is a key to their practical application in design.

The largest and most dominant is the *overstory tree* (the tallest of the natural forms, reaching a height of 100 feet (30.5 m) or more). Next is the *understory tree* (a natural form that must have the overstory form above it in order to survive); since it depends upon the shade of the overstory, the understory has difficulty existing and adapting to conditions other than those of its natural habitat. The *seedling tree* needs the protection of the understory to germinate and become a larger element of the natural environment. The *shrub* serves as a food and energy source for both animals and people, with *herbs* providing an additional protection for the soil. *Mosses and lichens* follow at the lower end of the life-form chain.

GEOGRAPHIC DISTRIBUTION FACTORS

The existence and distribution of a plant in a natural setting is subject to the "approval" of the environment that surrounds it.

There are two basic levels of distribution. *Macrodistribution* is geographic; plants at this level occur in a general region or pattern. *Microdistribution* is ecological, with species occurring only in certain kinds of environmental situations, for example, north-facing slopes or the edges of streams and lakes.

A few species of plants are found almost everywhere and are referred to as *cosmopolitan* species. Others, with restricted distribution, are found in only one area and are called *endemic* species. Plants restricted to a given region (such as eastern North America) are broad endemics and include such plants as the flowering dogwood (*Cornus florida*) and ponderosa pine (*Pinus ponderosa*). Those restricted to the microenvironments in a narrow geographic area are narrow endemics and include the isolated redwoods (*Sequoia sempervirens*) of California.

The presence or absence of a winter season separates

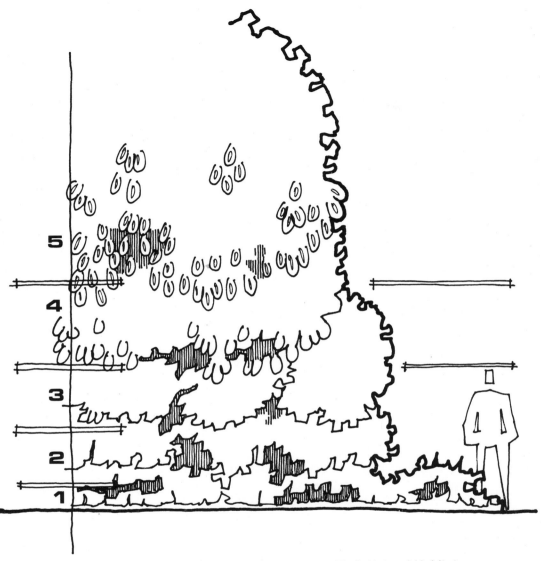

Figure 1–18. The Life Forms of Plants as They Occur in Their Natural Habitat

Form 1:   Mosses and lichens
Form 2:   Shrub zone
Form 3:   Seedling tree zone
Form 4:   Understory zone
Form 5:   Overstory zone

the distribution of plants into three groups. The first, *arctic-alpine* (harsh winter), is made up primarily of perennial herbs occurring as tundra plants. The second, *temperate,* is made up of widely distributed species genetically capable of producing individuals adapted to different climates. The third, *pantropical,* consists of species located throughout the tropics in cultivated areas.

TOLERANCE RANGE FACTORS

In studying the distribution of plants in terms of their selection as design elements, the factor of tolerance range will be one of the most important considerations. The tolerance range of an individual plant is that range of environmental conditions in which the plant can be grown and will reproduce. The greater the genetic variety in a plant species, the greater the tolerance range.

Tolerance range differs from ecological range in that the latter comprises a set of circumstances in which a plant actually does grow. For example, a species of plants may be tolerant to the conditions in Colorado but may only grow in New Mexico. This difference may lead to the introduction of a species into a new but compatible area and allow an expansion of its design capabilities. The ecological range of a plant is governed by its geographic or physical range; if a plant can travel to other areas, it has a potential geographic or physical range.

References Cited

1. Dice, Lee R. *Natural Communities.* University of Michigan Press, Ann Arbor, 1952.
2. Shelford, Victor E. *The Ecology of North America.* The University of Illinois Press, Urbana, 1963.
3. Spurr, Stephen H. and Burton V. Barnes. *Forest Ecology.* John Wiley and Sons, New York, 1964.
4. Watt, Kenneth E. F. *Ecology and Resource Management.* McGraw-Hill Book Company, New York, 1968.

2. DESIGN CONSIDERATIONS

The future health and survival of the natural landscape depends upon the design of an environment that is closely linked to its vegetative condition prior to destruction. This does not mean that continuous rows of red and yellow flowers are not attractive, because these materials do have a place in an artistic composition. It is to say, however, that the design of the natural landscape is critical if areas such as mine spoils, burned acreages, overused farmsteads, or public wilderness preserves are to be returned to their predamage condition.

The assumptions that a project team must make when undertaking the design of a natural landscape are numerous and varied. The conditions that exist both on and off the site are important factors that influence the selection of materials for the natural composition. The purposes of the project as envisioned by a client must be weighed against the capability of an area to fulfill the owner needs and objectives. Any size project, from a small residential planting to a large-scale mining spoil must be thoroughly evaluated in order to provide the design team with a pertinent and valuable resource upon which to base its decisions.

To design a natural landscape, a design team should first make a careful analysis of the site, using extensive, acceptable inventory and evaluation procedures. This effort should develop an informational base that will guide the decision-making process for the improvement of the site.

By paying careful attention to the soils, slopes, climates, vegetation, hydrology, and aesthetic factors of a project, immediate design considerations may be taken into account in the following areas.

CRITICAL VEGETATION

If the project site has been severely damaged by fire, flooding, or mechanical misuse, the immediate establishment of protective vegetation should be of the highest priority. This is usually the case where severe erosion or continuous site damage must be rapidly checked before other work can proceed. In doing so, a dilemma many face the design team: whether or not to use "introduced" or "native" plant species for this effort.

The guiding factor, at this point, should be site condition and control. Halt or reverse the destruction by whatever means available. Introduced or ornamental plant species may not have the long-term aesthetic effect desired for the project, but they may be the most practical choice for the immediate need. On sediment-producing, highly erodible areas such as mine spoils, highway cuts, or denuded gullies, this is an applicable design decision (Fig. 2-1).

In the specific selection of plant materials, it is important to remember the following:

Select a species that is adaptable to the site environment.

Select a species that can be easily removed after other plants have been established.

Avoid species that are subject to disease or damage from severe climate change.

Use a plant type that will intercept and check the movements of water or sand across the site.

It may also be necessary to support the use of plants with such features as diversion terraces, grade stabilization structures, or other drainageways to reverse especially severe conditions. It is good design to use these initially, but they should be removed before final revegetation efforts are concluded.

Temporary vegetation should be used on any damaged or denuded areas subject to continuous abuse for six months or more prior to the establishment of permanent vegetation. If the soil of the site is firm and not compacted, it may be smooth enough for planting if it has not been sealed by continuous rainfall. However, if it has been sealed or compacted, it should be worked to a depth of at least 4 inches (10 cm) prior to planting the temporary plant materials (Fig. 2-2).

A mass of plant materials that prevents severe soil erosion will, obviously, improve site conditions. Other factors, such as soil-improving species, should also be con-

Figure 2–1a. This highway right-of-way is a critical planting area requiring immediate action by the design team to prevent erosion (USDA-Soil Conservation Service)

Figure 2–1b. Rains and melting snows can quickly damage a site if a critical planting program is not adopted. (USDA-Soil Conservation Service)

Figure 2–1c. Soil netting may be used before planting operations begin in order to stabilize the site. (Courtesy of Jim Walls Company, Dallas, Texas)

Figure 2–1d. Grass seeds are not inhibited with the use of this soil netting. It will eventually decompose into needed organic matter. (Courtesy of Jim Walls Company, Dallas, Texas)

Figure 2–1e. This right-of-way was damaged by fire and is being prepared for an application of soil netting and grass seed. (Courtesy of Jim Walls Company, Dallas, Texas)

Figure 2–1f. After a few months, the natural grass seeds are developing to replace the netting material. (Courtesy of Jim Walls Company, Dallas, Texas)

sidered at the critical stage of planting. The best example of this design treatment would be legumes. These materials can be established within the initial program to rebuild lost soil nitrogen and prepare conditions for future planting requirements (Fig. 2-3).

The temporary materials for a project may be limited to the commercial availability of the geographic region. Some government agencies, state or national forest service nurseries, or even the USDA-Soil Conservation Service programs may be contacted in order to develop a site adequately. If it is necessary to collect the plant material, remember the factor of genetics. Collections should not

be made outside the geographic range of species (*see* Geographic Distribution Factors and Tolerance Range Factors).

EVALUATING THE SITE

The concept of *site carrying capacity* is useful as an aid in determining the quality of the natural landscape. This concept can be expressed in many ways, but here it is defined as the number of vegetative types per unit of project area that can be accommodated for any specific period of time, so that the natural characteristics of the

Figure 2–1g. One growing season following the damage by fire, the right-of-way is almost completely recovered. (Courtesy of Jim Walls Company, Dallas, Texas)

species and the quality of the designed environment are sustained indefinitely. Important to this concept is a defined management program so that the intrinsic value of the design intent can be fully realized by the project team.

Site carrying capacity is composed of two basic factors: resource capacity and management capacity. The *resource capacity* is the maximum level of use that can be exerted indefinitely on the natural plant components of the resource base without changing the characteristics of the vegetation. The natural vegetative value of a project may be too easily altered by man with the simple addi-

tion or modification of site structures or by accidental intervention in the natural vegetative processes. The *management capacity* is the maximum sustainable level of human use that can be exerted indefinitely without impairment of the natural vegetative systems. Plant materials that are either on or are to be placed on the project site have certain tolerance thresholds beyond which continued impacts upon them by outside forces (people) become unacceptable. Determination of the site carrying capacity for a design project must take into account the overall land use, the factor of development time, and the needs of the client program. If the natural landscape project is used for any purpose, this use must be considered in terms of resource and management determinations.

Management (or client) objectives must state the sought uses in terms of project integrity and character, and they must be applied to vegetative tolerance thresholds.

The major environmental characteristics of an area that influence the natural landscape may be divided into site, biological, and cultural components. Among the *site components* are location, size, and shape, topography, geology and soils, hydrology, climate, and physiography. *Biological components* principally comprise the plants and animals of the area. *Cultural components* include past and present land use, existing facilities, aesthetics, and historical attributes. One or more of these characteristics may be so important that it gives an area its particular value as a natural resource, but all these items need to be assessed to properly evaluate the potentials and limitations of a project site.

SITE COMPONENTS

The various site characteristics considered here are interrelated. They depend on each other for their origin and ap-

Figure 2-2. This project was first overgrazed by livestock, then suffered damage from range fires. The soil has become compacted and will retard the development of natural vegetation if not improved before planting operations begin. (USDA-Soil Conservation Service)

Figure 2-3. These sand hills have been damaged by livestock, shifting soils, and continuous high winds. Site-improving plants or mechanical soil nettings should be used to check the damage before future planting operations are begun. (USDA-Soil Conservation Service)

plication to the project. These components are discussed below in terms of their individuality but should be combined in various ways to make interpretations in terms of their impact on and relevance to the development of a natural landscape.

Location, Size, and Shape

It is important to have a complete and accurate description of a project area for location and identification purposes. A map showing the location of the site in relation to population centers, highways, flood zones, and major utility easements may be helpful in predicting future management strategies (Fig. 2-4).

A small project area will limit the vegetation types that can be selected for planting. Overcrowding from too many species will limit vegetative tolerance and is usually the first mistake a designer will make. Larger sites can tolerate more species without altering the character of the site (Fig. 2-5).

Narrow project sites may also limit the planting programs by reducing the mixing or blending of plant species for the natural composition. Some vegetative types need a large planting area for their initial introduction, which may require management programs to begin on off-site areas.

Topography

The surface features of an area, including the shape of the land and the distribution of water bodies (if present), are its most apparent physical aspects. A topographic map and a soil map are essential documents that portray these features. A standard U. S. Geological Survey 1:24,000-scale topographic quadrangle map may serve as a useful base. For more detailed studies, particularly of a small area, a large-scale soils or topographic map may be required (Fig. 2-6).

The topography may be classified and the land easily visualized in terms of the landforms that compose it. Among these, for example, may be an association of kinds of soils, valleys, terraces, plains, rolling hills, and subdued or rugged mountains. A small area may be entirely in one of these landform units or soil associations. A large area, on the other hand, may be divided into various landform types of soil associations that are more homogeneous in vegetative communities, each of which can be developed and managed in different ways.

The percentage of grade for the site is directly associated to soil depth. The more stable the slope, the deeper the soil in most cases. Grade will also influence the location and placement of materials because of exposure to light and air movement (Fig. 2-7).

Topography is also related to climate by its orientation. Site temperatures for species adaptation are lower on north- and northeast-facing slopes than on those facing south and west. Cooler temperatures will lower the evaporation of water from the plants, resulting in more for plant growth. However, lower temperatures may reduce the length of the growing season as well as increase the risk of frost damage.

Low areas such as valleys and draws will tend to have higher soil moisture and cooler temperatures. This may affect plant establishment and performance for the selected species (Fig. 2-8).

Slope orientation will expose various materials to prevailing winds in both summer and winter. Winds increase the availability of water to the plant, both from the soil and in the materials themselves.

The topographic analyzation of a project site should result in a graphic product that relates the following grade percentages: 0 to 3; 3 to 8; 8 to 15; 15 to 25; and 25 percent or higher.

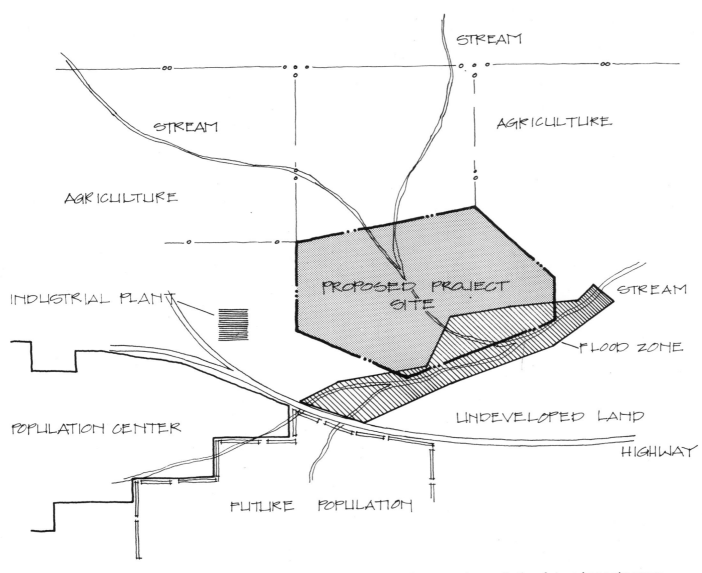

STREAM

STREAM

AGRICULTURE

AGRICULTURE

PROPOSED PROJECT SITE

INDUSTRIAL PLANT

STREAM

FLOOD ZONE

POPULATION CENTER

UNDEVELOPED LAND

HIGHWAY

FUTURE POPULATION

Figure 2-4. An accurate site location map will assist the design team in predicting future impacts upon the natural landscape project. Runoff from agricultural areas may wash herbicides onto the project. An industrial facility may inject airborne pollutants. Population centers, highways, and future housing developments may subject the site to unwanted human impact.

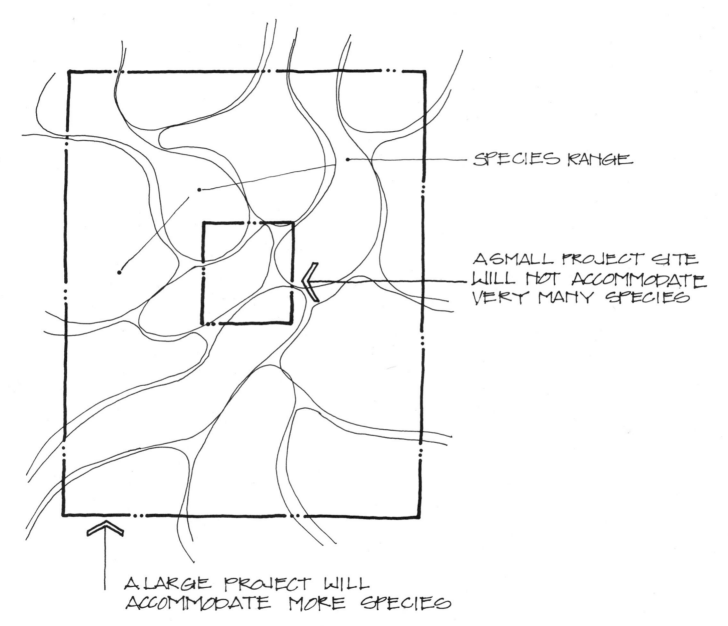

SPECIES RANGE

A SMALL PROJECT SITE
WILL NOT ACCOMMODATE
VERY MANY SPECIES

A LARGE PROJECT WILL
ACCOMMODATE MORE SPECIES

Figure 2-5.

Figure 2–6. The topography of this project site reveals the microclimates of the various vegetative communities, from grasses to understory and canopy trees. (USDA-Soil Conservation Service)

Figure 2–7. Typical vegetative cover on loam soils 2 to 60 percent slope. One soil type is on the level areas, another on the canyon sides. (USDA-Soil Conservation Service)

Figure 2–8. Slope orientation is associated to plant selection by controlling the amount of moisture and light reaching the vegetative communities. (USDA-Soil Conservation Service)

Geology and Soils

The geologic formations and kinds of soils that underlie an area play a very important role in determining how the area may be designed and the limitations that must be placed on its use. Geologic and soils studies should be undertaken (if they have not already been done) to gather the basic data needed to make the necessary evaluations of the land for determining appropriate design intent (Fig. 2-9).

Many kinds of soils and geologic materials are more suitable for some purposes than for others, and a knowledge of the distribution of these characteristics will aid in the selection of suitable plants and in the design and maintenance of required management principles that best fit natural conditions. Foundation and excavation conditions, for example, vary with the kind of soil and the depth to bedrock. Clayey soils generally have lower bearing capacity for structures than coarse-grained soils or rocks do and are especially hazardous when they become wet; shallow bedrock provides solid foundations but requires more expensive methods of excavation. A combination of slope of the ground and kind of soil or structure and type of rock provides valuable clues as to the potential stability of the ground or of excavations such as for roads and buildings. Soil wetness, soil flooding, and the ability of the soil to absorb sewage and other wastes can be determined from a knowledge of the kind of soil and of the surficial geologic deposits found in an area.

The effective depth of the soil surface is a very important factor. It is the area that is either occupied or has the capability of being occupied by the plant material

Figure 2-9. Severe erosion on this project site has exposed the bedrock that will prove hazardous to the future design and planting operations. (USDA-Soil Conservation Service)

selected for a design project. Bedrock near the surface will prevent the use of certain species, while a soil susceptible to high water tables during the growing season will limit root growth. A barrier of hard, coarse soil may limit root penetration for expanded plant sizes (Figs. 2-10 and 2-11).

Some plants require acid soils, some alkaline, while some are tolerant to a wide range of pH. Extremely high pH may restrict the availability of nutrients. Extremely low pH may release toxic substances that will limit plant growth or terminate it altogether. Mine spoils are an excellent example of high-risk, toxic areas.

Common to arid and semiarid areas is salinity. This will limit plant growth unless sufficient water is available for leaching. Soils derived from magnesium iron silicates are called *serpentine* and are usually sterile and unproductive. What vegetation that does occur on the serpentine base is in striking contrast to adjacent species. Regardless of the site, an extensive soil analysis should be made to determine future nutrient requirements for plant growth.

Although basic soil and geologic maps contain data to make evaluations such as those indicated above, such data may be more rapidly grasped if it is presented

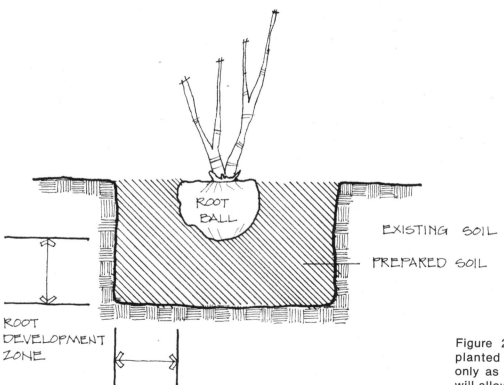

Figure 2-10. The roots of the planted materials will expand only as far as the project soils will allow.

Figure 2–11a. The effective depth of this soil may inhibit the root growth of some plant species. (USDA-Soil Conservation Service)

Figure 2–11b. The effective depth of this soil will allow roots to penetrate for proper plant growth. (USDA-Soil Conservation Service)

separately in maps that interpret the basic data for specific purposes. Both the Soil Conservation Service and the U. S. Geologic Survey—as well as other groups outside the federal government—have produced such interpretive maps. These maps are made in such a way that they may be readily understood by people not trained in specialties like geology and soil science. With such maps, designers and managers can avoid uses that are incompatible with the capabilities of the soil or rock formations. Listed below are some of the types of maps that are available. Not all are listed here, and not all of the maps listed need be made for any one project area. The types selected would depend on the specific project under consideration. Some of the maps listed are essentially different versions of the same map, with emphases appropriate to characteristics of different areas.

Depth of bedrock (thickness of soil and unconsolidated deposits)
Elevation of bedrock surface
Thickness of clay (or some other significant formation)
Lithology (rock type)
Texture of soil (particle size)
Clay content of soil
Stoniness of soil
Droughtiness of soil (indicative of need for irrigation)
Permeability of soil and/or rocks
Soil wetness (Fig. 2-12)
Soil productivity for different plants
Soil limitations for specific recreation uses
Absorptive capacity (suitability for waste disposal)
Suitability for impounding water
Shrink pressure potential of soil (expansive clays)
Soil susceptibility to frost heave
Soil bearing qualities
Limitations for excavation
Geologic hazards

Steepness of slope and slope stability
Susceptibility to landsliding
Erodibility of soils and/or geologic materials
Seismic susceptibility
pH rating

Hydrology

In the design and management of a natural landscape, it is essential to have an inventory of the quantity and quality of the water resources in or available to the area, as these will influence significantly the carrying capacity of the site and the management practice used. The size, depth, location, and quality of surface bodies of water directly influence the choice of vegetation types. Water available for irrigation can improve natural vegetation and, as a result, increase the tolerance thresholds of some vegetative species. Introduction of available water, however, can also fundamentally change the quality and character of the existing vegetation.

Data, including maps as appropriate, should be obtained and evaluated for the following items (Fig. 2-13):

Drainage areas
Potential for flooding, including frequency and duration
Low flow of streams
Sediment load of streams
Maximum concentration of dissolved solids in surface water
Amount and quality of surface runoff
Depth of surface water bodies
Potential reservoir sites
Availability of ground water
Location wells and test holes
Depth to water table (Fig. 2-14)
Elevation of water table

Elevation of piezometric surface (level to which water in wells will rise, seasonal water table)
Thickness of saturated materials
Quality of ground water
Ground-water recharge areas

Water is the element that helps the plant maintain cell function and to transport nutrients. It is always present in the atmosphere in the form of vapor. If it is important for water to reach the lower levels of plants on the site, then conifers should not be used as overstory, because they trap more water than do deciduous varieties. Air movement will affect water evaporation from plants and must be obstructed from some species (Fig. 2-15).

Figure 2–12. Some plant species can be temporarily retained or installed to help trap winter snows to increase soil moisture for spring planting operations. (USDA-Soil Conservation Service)

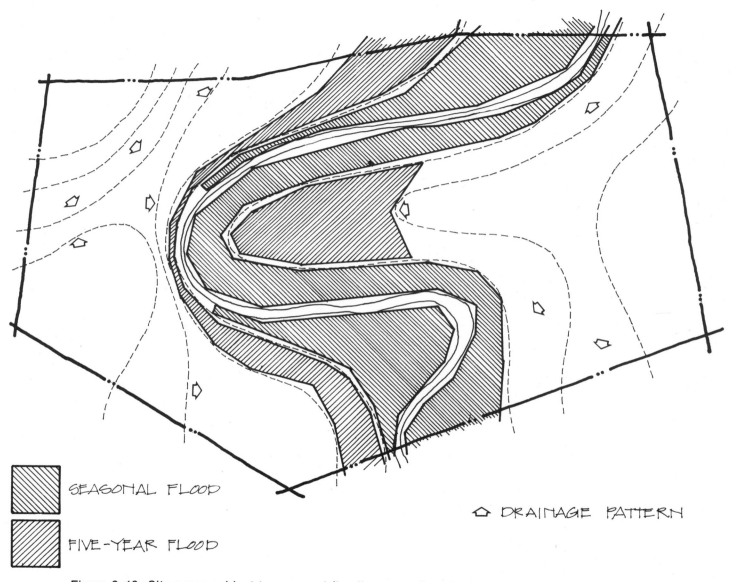

SEASONAL FLOOD

FIVE-YEAR FLOOD

△ DRAINAGE PATTERN

Figure 2–13. Site areas subject to seasonal flooding as well as those portions of the site within a five-year flood frequency should be studied. Drainage patterns are also important for the correct placement of some plant species.

38

Figure 2–14. The depth of the water table on this site is very shallow, as indicated by these surface pockets. (USDA-Soil Conservation Service)

Figure 2–15. Many plant species will be directly associated to water on the site. This project area has numerous species that have developed into microcommunities of a larger ecological zone. (USDA-Soil Conservation Service)

Site climate is obviously related to plant growth and to the quantity of the existing vegetative cover. The amount and duration of precipitation and the fluctuations of temperature are critical. Plant species are genetically adapted to their site by these factors, and the changing of the climate may limit or extend a specific plants use as a design element.

Basic climate data that influence the site carrying capacity and use of a natural landscape project include: average monthly temperature and precipitation; maximum daily, monthly, and annual temperature range; number of days with snow cover; number of frost-free days; annual flood cycles and flood levels; likelihood of tornadoes, hurricanes, other intense storms, and fog; average monthly humidity and wind velocity; and number of days per month when the sky is clear, partly cloudy, or cloudy. Short-term climatic trends should also be taken into account. Some specific hazards to natural vegetation that are related to climate are flash floods, polluted air, and very dry conditions which may influence fire.

Light and heat are two of the most important climate factors that are directly available to the plant. Light is the source of energy for photosynthesis, while heat is the energy source for the plants' metabolic processes.

The quality of light that will reach the understory will depend upon the density of the canopy. Growth for plants is directly related to their rate of photosynthesis. The failure of seedlings under the existing canopy of a site may be associated with low light levels from above which may create a fungal attack, even on the more shade-tolerant species (Fig. 2-16).

Root growth in larger plantings will be greatly impaired by poor light situations as well as the structure of the overall plant canopy. Too much shade during important periods of development may cause the plant to be easily damaged during severe ice or wind storms (Fig. 2-17).

40

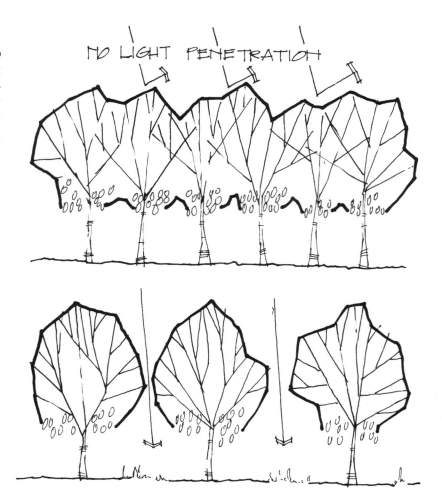

NO LIGHT PENETRATION

LIGHT PENETRATION FOR SEEDLINGS

Figure 2-16. Reducing the density of the canopy will aid in the development of understory trees and shrubs.

Heat, or temperature, is a factor when it fluctuates radically, causing injury to plant tissue. Site topography and the direction of the winds will also influence the tem-

Figure 2-17. Aided by a thick layer of pine needles, this understory vegetation has been limited to a thin stand of sedge and an occasional grass plant due to limited light. (USDA-Soil Conservation Service)

become ground terminals of lightning discharges, damaging other nearby plants.

Physiography

The physiographic elements are those natural impediments that may inhibit the attainment of certain types of management programs. Such things as earthquake faults, flash-flood zones, areas susceptible to violent storms, areas of unusually high water table, or critical wildlife habitats may be just a few elements to consider before developing the natural landscape.

BIOLOGICAL COMPONENTS

Existing Vegetative Spectrum

The type, species, location, size, and density of existing vegetation have a tremendous effect on the selection of design materials and the future carrying capacity of the site. A designer should make a careful analysis of all existing vegetation that is present on a project area. The abundance of the species, their size, and their location will indicate the very nature of the systems.

Because trees are long-lived and easily identifiable in all seasons, they are the first that should be studied. Some species, such as the black walnut, the white ash, and the yellow poplar, grow best on moist, well-drained soil. Understory species often have a more restricted ecological tolerance than does the canopy layer and may prove to be useful in site studies.

In all cases, the plants should be related to their requirements for moisture, soil, light, and association with the successional stage. Remember, however, the factors of growth competition and past events such as drought, fire, and insect damage will influence the quantity and size of the materials.

perature of the site. Some plants may require one temperature at night and another during the day. Some planted seedlings are able to withstand lower temperatures and avoid injury because of lowered transpiration.

Atmospheric pollutants will quickly destroy any existing or introduced plant material. Whether from the air or from soil leaching, damage can be noticed in inhibited sexual reproduction, revegetation following a fire, poor seedling growth, or even death.

Ice, wind storms, and lightning account for many of the mechanical factors in design consideration. These conditions can terminate the life of a plant or make it subject to diseases or insects. Large exposed trees on a site may

41

Specific events or stages of vegetative development should be noted, with a careful on-site analysis of the following:

1. *Pioneer or invader species.* These plant types are usually the first to establish themselves on a disturbed site. They are the more aggressive of the varieties and can grow on a soil less capable of supporting stronger plants. If extensive soil restoration is not possible immediately, these materials make excellent choices for an initial planting program (Fig. 2-18).
2. *Transitional species.* These plants follow the pioneer varieties and will remain until a more dominant material emerges (Fig. 2-19).
3. *Subclimax and climax species.* These plants represent the final stage in the successional process. They require a more nutrient soil and a more stable climate condition.
4. *Adjacent site vegetation.* The vegetative types on the opposite areas of a project may indicate a "direction" for the establishment of new vegetative communities. The direction of winds and the movement of surface water may allow seeds to be dispensed onto a project, allowing for natural revegetative techniques. If this natural technique is used, however, a great amount of time will be needed to reach the final objective (Fig. 2-20).

Wildlife Considerations

It is important for the project team to consider the type, location, and habitat of the existing wildlife of a natural area. These species and those that may be attracted to the finished site will influence the overall carrying capacity of the vegetative communities. For example, the number of deer on or near a project depends upon the abundance of suitable food and cover plants within their habitat range. If a planting program increases the food and cover materials, the deer population may increase or be attracted to the new site. This may, in turn, exert new pressures on the tolerance thresholds of the vegetation components (Fig. 2-21).

Aerial photographs, notes from on-site inspections, vegetation type maps, and wildlife species range maps may be utilized in the evaluation of wildlife components. The primary objective should be to preserve (or to attract back) a representative segment of the project fauna and the habitat critical to its continued existance. Important considerations should be plantings that influence diversity and abundance of food supplies; presence of water; availability of den and nest sites; and cover.

CULTURAL COMPONENTS

Past and Present Land Use

The type, location, and extent of the different uses, past and present, of a site are important for evaluating present and potential carrying capacity of the site. Maps showing the location of these uses can be part of the first step in evaluating present and potential design consideration for specific sites.

Existing Man-made Facilities

To determine the capacity of an area to support natural vegetative considerations, it is essential that an inventory be made of present facilities. This includes number, size, and capacity of utilities (especially those underground), roads, buildings, recreational facilities, and structures. Such things as farm dwellings, residences, railway facilities, and overhead transmission lines should be graphically portrayed for consideration during the design process.

Figure 2–18. These Chinese elms have invaded this grassland area within six years after seeding operations were completed. (USDA-Soil Conservation Service)

Figure 2–19. A mixture of transitional species and subclimax species are found throughout this project site. (USDA-Soil Conservation Service)

43

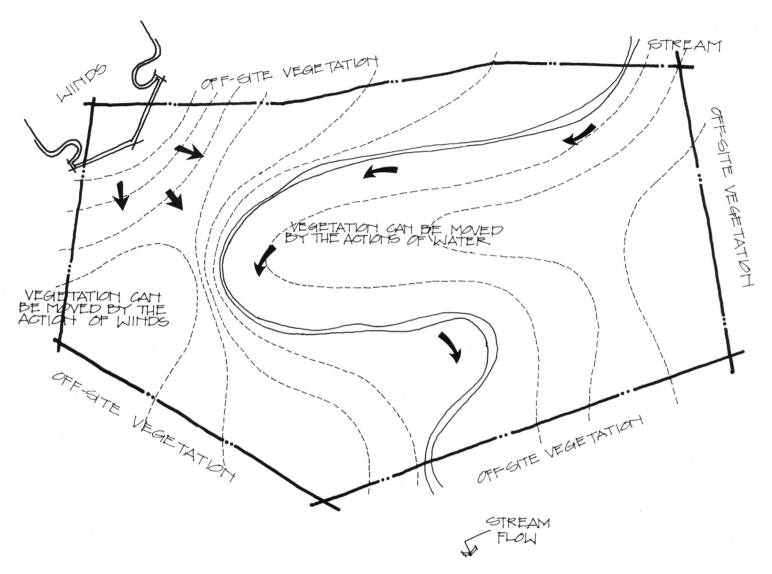

Figure 2–20. The *direction* of vegetation movement will help determine which natural processes are currently underway on the project site.

Figure 2-21. The creation of wildlife habitats within the natural landscape project should be an important intent of the design team. (USDA-Soil Conservation Service)

In evaluating the existing facilities component, conclusions should be based upon the direct or indirect relationship man has had or will have upon the future character of the site. In this context, it should be related to the physical, permanent developments, structures, or conditions that will influence the choice and application of natural vegetation communities.

Aesthetics

This aspect usually depends upon landform diversity, vegetative pattern, spatial definition, views, vistas, and overall site image. Specific considerations during the design process should be existing scenic vistas; orientation vistas; and overall scenic quality.

The primary objective is to preserve the existing areas of natural scenic beauty within the project site. Information used to evaluate the aesthetics may be obtained from aerial photographs, color slides, and detailed on-site inspections. Although each member of a planning team may have different interpretations of the aesthetic quality of a project, the following criteria may be used:

1. *High aesthetic quality.* These are portions of the site that possess unique beauty in their immediate proximity.
2. *Medium aesthetic quality.* From these portions of the site views or vistas that have a scenic quality may be seen.
3. *Low aesthetic quality.* These portions of the site appear scenic when seen from a distance but may or may not have unique beauty in their immediate vicinity.

Historical Attributes

Every project area generally has significant historical qualities. A specific knowledge of the exact location on the site and the importance of these qualities is a major consideration for the design team. Some historical features might include historic trails, passageways, structures, or sites that may be located within the project boundaries.

A PROCESS FOR DESIGNING THE NATURAL LANDSCAPE

Current trends in the landscape industry favor a more naturalistic arrangement of ornamental plant materials. And, although the natural plant spectrum for such a prac-

45

tice is inadequate, it is a positive turn in the development of both large- and small-scale landscape environments.

The large-scale natural landscape will save installation time and reduce equipment costs, and it will be more conducive to energy conservation than is the traditional ornamental garden. Developers of major housing areas and residential neighborhoods are beginning to realize that the natural landscape will offer more benefits for the long-term investment and a greater return on their monetary resources. The small-scale residential project will benefit from reduced installation fees, long-term maintenance expenditures, especially out of shrinking household budgets. The residential structure may be more easily blended with its surroundings for a more visually pleasing environment.

Because of the environmental benefits and the developmental advantages of a natural composition, it is important to consider a process that might be employed to design the final product. For the large-scale site, the following steps may be applicable.

Step One: Preplanning

Data Investigation/Collection

This is the information-collecting phase when the designer begins to accumulate the volumes of technical data needed to support the conclusions and judgments of the development team. Information that should be collected includes—but is not limited to—the following:

1. *Base maps.* These should include the most recent county and state maps, aerial photos, contour maps, and maps of adjacent property. For projects that may be in or near urban areas, a zoning map should be included.
2. *Soil surveys.* Current soil data should be obtained

from local county agricultural agents or the nearest Soil Conservation Service district office. An additional source for this information may be a state highway department.

3. *Weather data.* Information on rainfall, temperature and humidity fluctuation, winds, and seasonal disturbances should be collected. The National Weather Service is the best source for this information.
4. *Utilities.* A thorough determination of available utilities that may be needed to service the support facilities or installation operations is important in this step. Items to be studied should include water (size, length of service, location) and electricity.
5. *Land documents.* Study the deeds to the property site and inspect the fine print that may contain provisions for easements. It could prove embarrassing if a right-of-way through the site is overlooked.
6. *Water.* For water features that exist on the site, a designer should study the conservation pool and flood frequencies. For streams, collect data concerning flooding and watershed. For bay and gulf areas, check tide fluctuations and shoreline erosion.

The following outline will summarize the research that is needed.

I. Physical Information
   A. Property Data
      1. *Topographic map.* This should illustrate the contour lines of existing slopes and site features that may influence the proposed project.
      2. *Boundary lines.* The limits of the design project as well as the property lines of the client

program are important factors of this research step.

3. *Slope analysis.* Determine the percentage and orientation of the slope on the site.
4. *Hydrology.* Is there a source of water (natural or artificial) on the site.
5. *Climate.* What are the temperature, rainfall, and humidity ranges. What are the directions of seasonal winds.
6. *Soils.* The surface and subsurface elements should be determined, with their relationship to plant materials defined.
7. *Existing plants.* Will these materials complement or interfere with the goals of the project.
8. *Adjacent structures.* Will these features relate to the projected intent.

B. Utility Data
1. *Availability.* What is the source of potential facilities serving the site.
2. *Location on site.* Where are these elements as they relate to the site (above and below ground).
3. *Size and capacity.* Will the utilities meet the present and future needs of the project.

II. Historical Information
A. Abstracts. Search the titles and land data base for issues that may have a bearing on the future use of the site.
B. Easements. Determine the development restrictions of your site area.
C. Historical Significant Data. These include the past and present land usage, zoning growth, and restrictions and preservation requirements.

Site Verification

The on-site investigation is conducted by the project team to verify the data collected and investigated during the previous exercise.

1. *Existing facilities.* Make an accurate record of the condition of any structure or facility that may exist on the project site. Make floor plans of existing buildings and layouts of other facilities.
2. *Verification of soils.* Check to see if the information obtained from the Soil Conservation Service is accurate. This verification should contain pertinent soil information that will directly affect the selection and placement of vegetation.
3. *Biological survey.* This investigation usually begins with an overall evaluation of the site as a landscape resource. Existing vegetative types, the location of habitat for any rare or endangered species, the location and description of ecologically sensitive communities, and the location of areas where concentrated human use will be least detrimental to vegetative habitat should be carefully delineated.
4. *Historical features.* This section includes information on the historical significance of the project site and an evaluation of any areas that might be affected by development.
5. *Utilities system.* This report should outline the availability of utilities that would be needed for the installation and maintenance of vegetation communities.

Step Two: Develop Site Capacities

The most honorable of goals may terminate abruptly if the site considered for development cannot support the wishes or desires of a client. This important research step should examine the capabilities of the site to withstand

47

these pressures. The capacity of each component should, therefore, be expressed in the form of a values map that would indicate the limitations by which the natural landscape project could be developed. Refer to the sections on site, biological, and cultural components to determine the needed criteria.

Step Three: Determine Development Limitations

From the information supplied by the client regarding the intent of the project, the designer should be able to set forth specific site limitations when this "intent" is compared to the site capacity. Three alternatives therefore can be summarized at this juncture in the process. First, all of the client issues can be obtained by this site. Second, a portion of the issues can be obtained with minor alterations in either the client program or site features. Third, none of the issues can be met without major or costly modifications of client program or site features. It is at this phase of the process that the designer and/or client should determine whether or not the project should be continued or abandoned.

Step Four: Developing the Planting Plans

Essentially, there are two types of planting plans that may be used for the development of a natural landscape. The first is the *critical areas plan,* which establishes the initial plantings to repair any site damage that may have occurred before the project began. The second is the *phased plan,* which provides the completed project program based upon the original design intent.

The critical planting of vegetation to repair a damaged site is the most important step in the development process. Although this procedure is the first phase of any planting operation, it should be guided by a separate planting plan. This will allow for a more comprehensive restoration effort on the site and will prevent further deterioration from a prolonged planning process.

During the site inventory and resource analysis phases of the design operations, the soils conditions map will be one of the most important products used to aid in critical planting. From this component, the designer should determine which soils are deficient in nutrients and which are currently suitable for planting. Some will require only minimum treatment, while others may need to be excavated and replaced (Fig. 2-22).

The damaged site conditions should be studied separately and analyzed on the basis of their relationship to the overall planting program. Destruction by severe erosion, chemical spills, trash dumps, or contaminated soils should be corrected in this first-phase operation to insure future planting compatability (Figs. 2-23 and 2-24).

After the site conditions analysis is completed, it should be compared to the soils conditions for a resulting *critical areas map* (Fig. 2-25). This document will determine where the most important development resources should be placed on the site. From this indication, the designer can now begin the *critical areas planting plan* and the subsequent *phased planting plan* (Figs. 2-26 and 2-27).

In order to implement the specific design intent of a client or client group, a design should rely upon the basic architectural characteristics of the plant materials within the ornamental spectrum. Plant form, color, texture, and scale will not change appreciably from an ornamental project to a natural composition. What does change is the application of the plant materials. Uses for vegetative masses must avoid drastic variations from the natural *life forms* or current *successional stage.* Doing so will jeopardize the value of the project composition as a representative of the natural landscape.

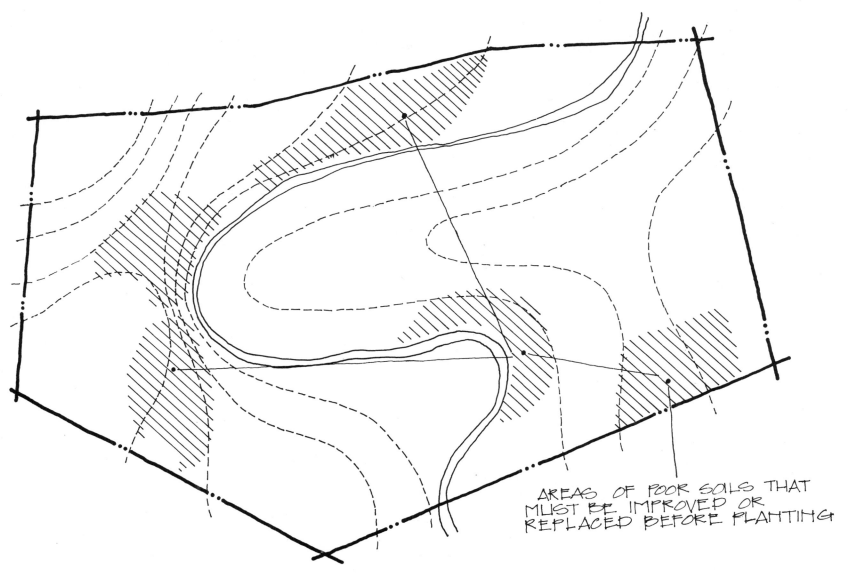

AREAS OF POOR SOILS THAT
MUST BE IMPROVED OR
REPLACED BEFORE PLANTING

Figure 2-22. The most critical soil deficiencies should be noted during the first phase of the planting design. If all the site soils are in poor condition, this mapping component may not be necessary.

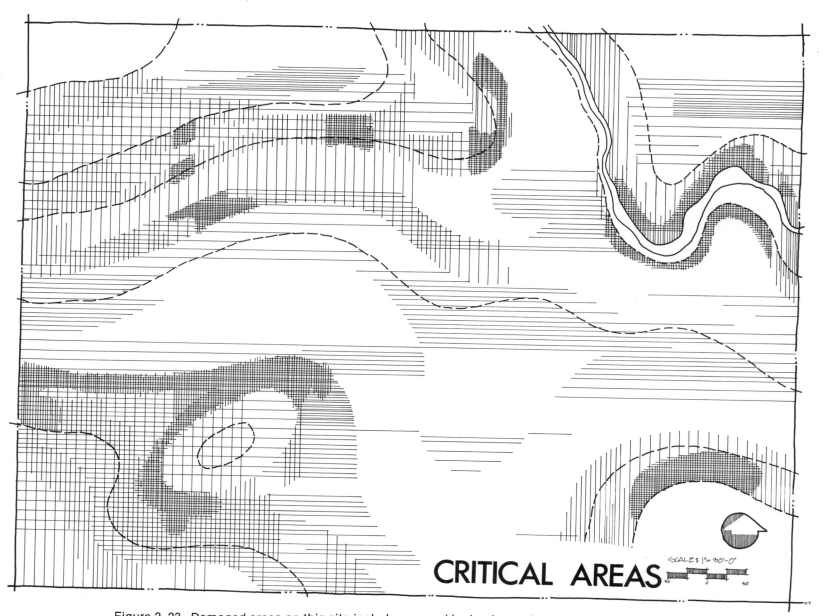

CRITICAL AREAS

SCALE: 1" = 30'-0"

Figure 2-23. Damaged areas on this site include exposed bedrock, erosion, fire damage, and a chemical spill. These are the portions of the site that will probably require a mechanical solution before planting begins.

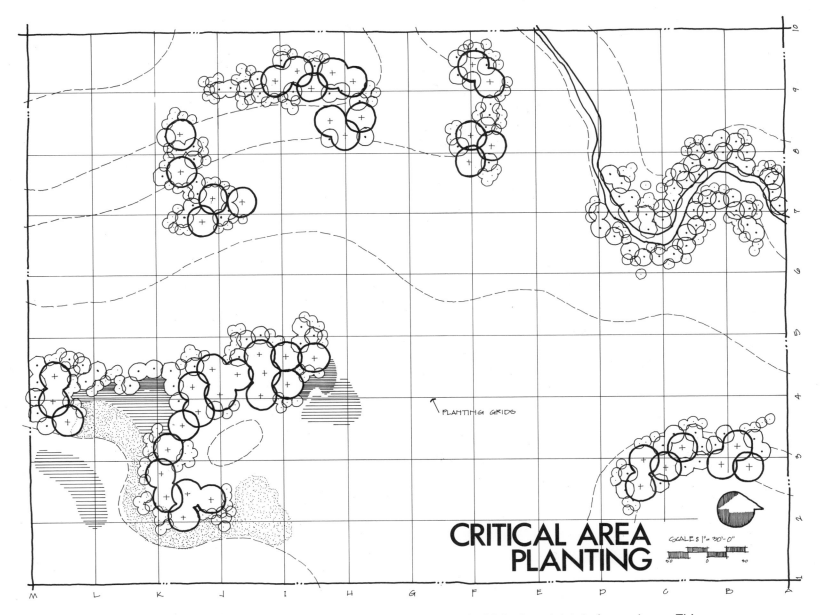

CRITICAL AREA
PLANTING

PLANTING GRIDS

SCALES 1" = 30'-0"

Figure 2–24. Unfortunately, too many sites will be cluttered with junk and debris from misuse. This site will require extensive reconstruction for this drainageway as well as an extensive critical planting program. (Courtesy USDA-Soil Conservation Service)

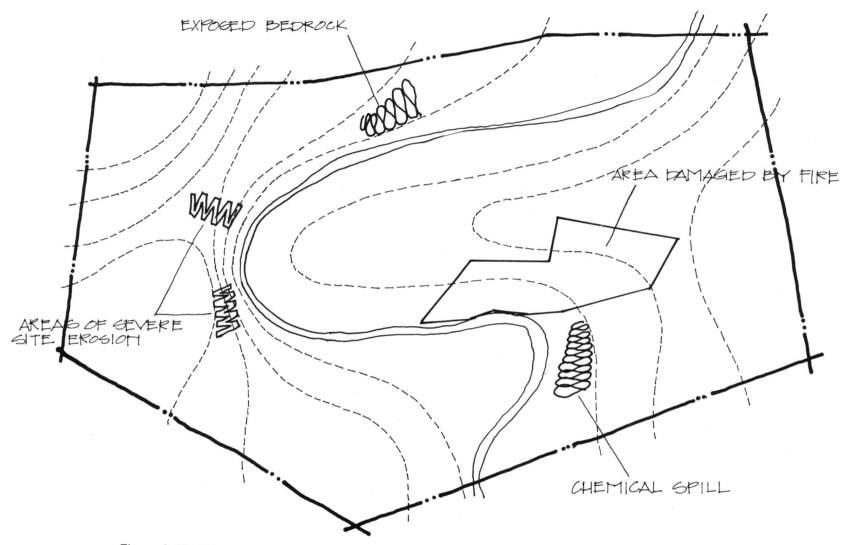

EXPOSED BEDROCK

AREA DAMAGED BY FIRE

AREAS OF SEVERE
SITE EROSION

CHEMICAL SPILL

Figure 2-25. This map represents the critical areas of the site that should be treated and planted to stabilize the project for future development. The darker areas are damage zones overlayed onto a soils conditions map.

52

Figure 2–26. The *critical areas planting* plan should stabilize the damaged conditions of the site and allow phased operations to begin. Planting grids may be used on the site to provide for a more accurate placement of materials.

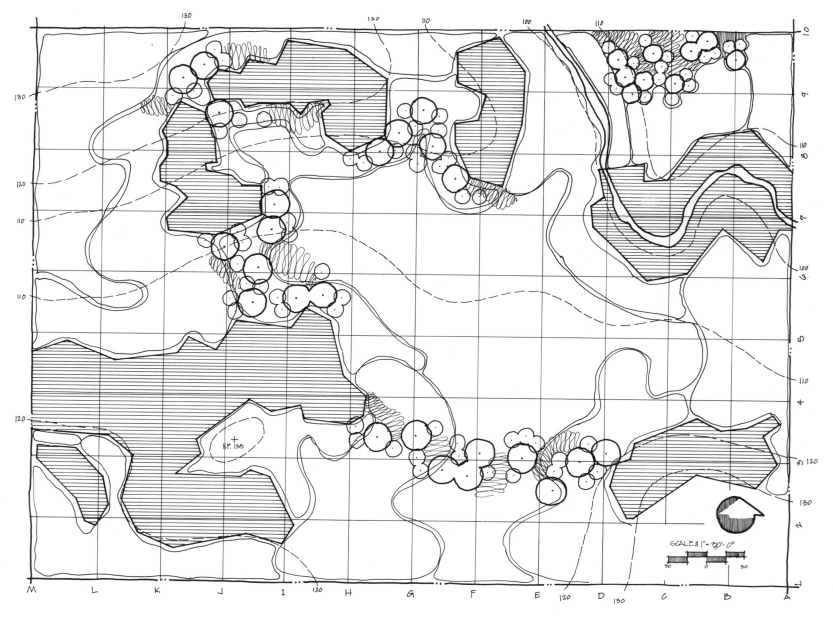

Figure 2-27. Phased planting plan.

Realizing, however, that the majority of projects will involve human impact upon the site, the following techniques may be used to minimize this impact and create a more harmonious balance between the site and the user (Figs. 2-28 to 2-35).

There is little variation between the large-scale critical or phased planting plans and the small-scale residential project. The design steps are similar in scope and, essentially, lead to the same conclusions. A slight modification in the preplanning step might be applicable, however, to include the investigation of the following:

The desirable or undesirable views from the site
The direction of sunrise and sunset for exposure requirements
The portions of the site shaded by the structure
The lanes or channels of pedestrian access needed for the site
A listing of the client's needs and desires in regard to the way they wish to use the spaces

Following the completion of the preplanning investigations, the outdoor space can be organized into primary use areas, which include (Fig. 2-36):

1. *Public area.* This encompasses the front entrance to the house, including driveway, walks, and front entry area.
2. *Utility area.* This includes outdoor work areas, such as the garden, clothesline, trash cans, tool storage, dog pen, recreation equipment, etc.
3. *Private area.* This is the outdoor living area, including the patio, outdoor cooking area, and flower garden.

From these general spaces, primary use areas can be developed that will help determine the amount of space needed for each client activity (Fig. 2-37). Because there is a more common use and need for direct access between some spaces and others, consider the relationships between the activity areas and the rooms of the house when arranging these outdoor areas.

Plant masses can now be organized on the site to fulfill the preliminary planting objectives of the client program. While canopy masses tend to create ceilings or high walls in the residential composition, shrub masses provide walls at a height more to human scale. Because of this, shrub masses are an effective means of defining and seperating spaces in the setting. Most natural shrub masses, however, require more room to function as a design element than do typical ornamental species. Of specific importance are the screen, baffle, and barrier mass (Figs. 2-38 to 2-41).

Keeping the functional uses and design principles in mind, determine the plant types that will occupy the planting areas established during the previous steps. Indicate the proposed surface area on the site, determine the specific plant material species that will meet the design requirements, and then select the plants needed for the design. For each plant, you should remember:

Height and spread at maturity
Growth habit
Time it will bloom and the color of its flowers
The time and color of its fruit
The amount of light, water, and temperature it needs
The texture and depth of the soil it needs
Other plants or animals it needs for association

Once the species have been chosen for planting, they should be delineated according to their mature spread. Plants that grow naturally in clusters, or thickets, may be drawn as a mass rather than as individuals. The nature of the planting design and personal preference of the designer will determine which drafting technique to use. Figures 2–42 through 2–44 show a typical residential planting plan, and plant list, as well as a design for handling walkways.

55

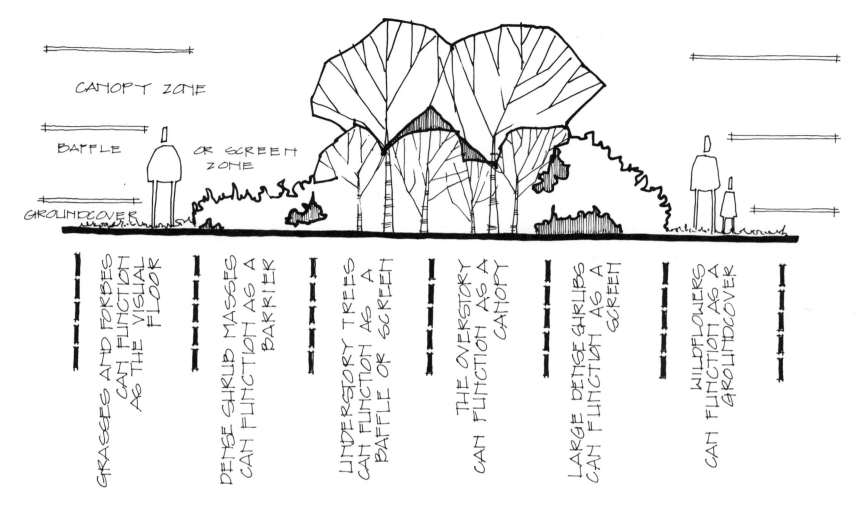

CANOPY ZONE

BAFFLE OR SCREEN ZONE

GROUNDCOVER

GRASSES AND FORBES CAN FUNCTION AS THE VISUAL FLOOR

DENSE SHRUB MASSES CAN FUNCTION AS A BARRIER

UNDERSTORY TREES CAN FUNCTION AS A BAFFLE OR SCREEN

THE OVERSTORY CAN FUNCTION AS A CANOPY

LARGE DENSE SHRUBS CAN FUNCTION AS A SCREEN

WILDFLOWERS CAN FUNCTION AS A GROUNDCOVER

Figure 2-28. The five architectural forms of plant materials can be easily recreated in the natural landscape if different planting space is available.

Figure 2-29. A canopy/groundcover/screen combination was employed here to enhance the visitor experience next to this meadow of wildflowers. (Courtesy of Johnson, Johnson, and Roy, Inc,. Ann Arbor, Michigan).

Figure 2-30. The combination of a canopy, screen, barrier, baffle, and ground cover can be used in one plant mass in the natural landscape. (Courtesy of Johnson, Johnson and Roy, Inc., Ann Arbor. Michigan)

Figure 2-31. The open spaces of this park are supported by masses of natural vegetation to create vistas for increased visual experiences. (Courtesy of Johnson, Johnson and Roy, Inc., Ann Arbor, Michigan)

Figure 2-32. The screen function of the natural mass may be achieved if the planting space is sufficient. (Courtesy of Johnson, Johnson and Roy, Inc., Ann Arbor, Michigan)

Figure 2–33. A mixture of overstory, understory, and small shrubs blends into this wildflower meadow to create a functional open space. Straight or intersecting lines should not be used in creating the natural landscape. (Courtesy of Johnson, Johnson, & Roy, Inc., Ann Arbor, Michigan)

Figure 2–34. Vehicular rights-of-way can support native vegetation communities without distracting from the purpose of the roadway. It is not only more practical but less expensive to use natural vegetation for this purpose. (Courtesy of Johnson, Johnson, and Roy, Inc., Ann Arbor, Michigan)

59

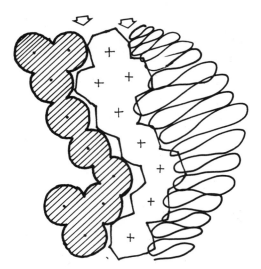

THE TRANSITIONAL ZONE OF AN ORNAMENTAL COMPOSITION

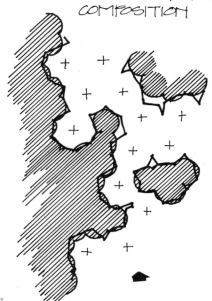

THE TRANSITIONAL ZONE OF A NATIVE COMPOSITION

Figure 2–35. The transitional zone between different plant species in the natural landscape is less defined than it is in the ornamental setting. It should be difficult to determine where one species ends and another one begins.

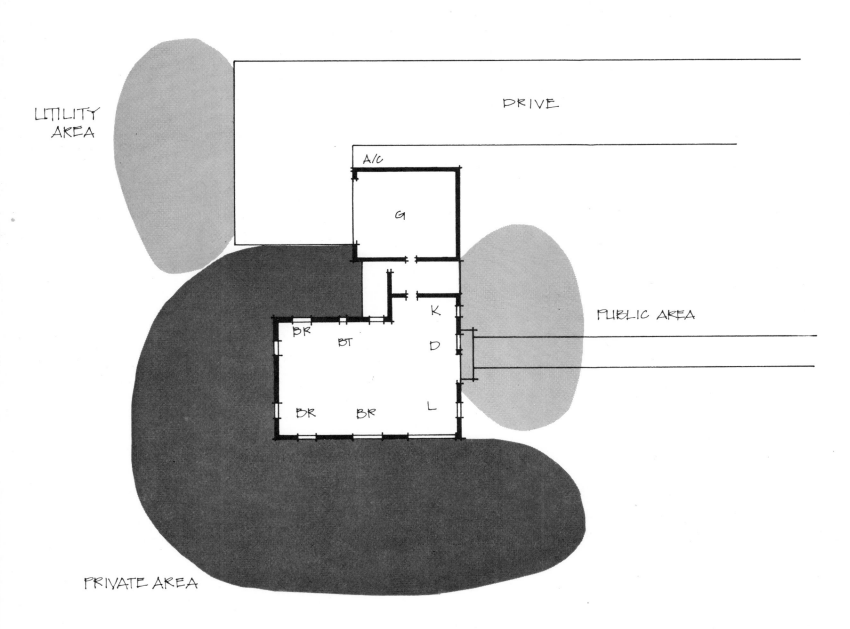

UTILITY AREA

DRIVE

A/c

G

PUBLIC AREA

K

BR
BT
D

BR   BR   L

PRIVATE AREA

Figure 2–36. These general-use areas represent a typical arrangement for a residential space. They will help define the specific associations of masses to site uses that are determined in later steps.

61

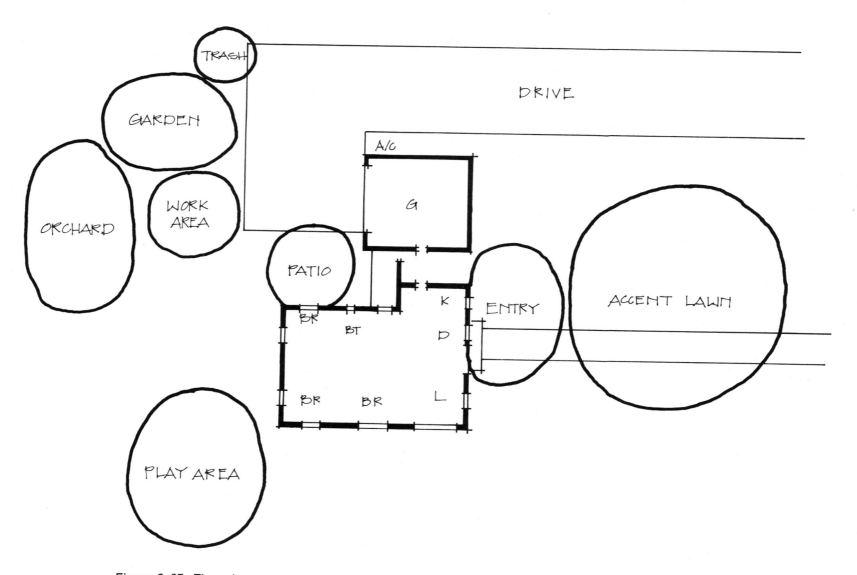

Figure 2-37. The primary use areas are established from the "design intent" resulting from the client needs and desires.

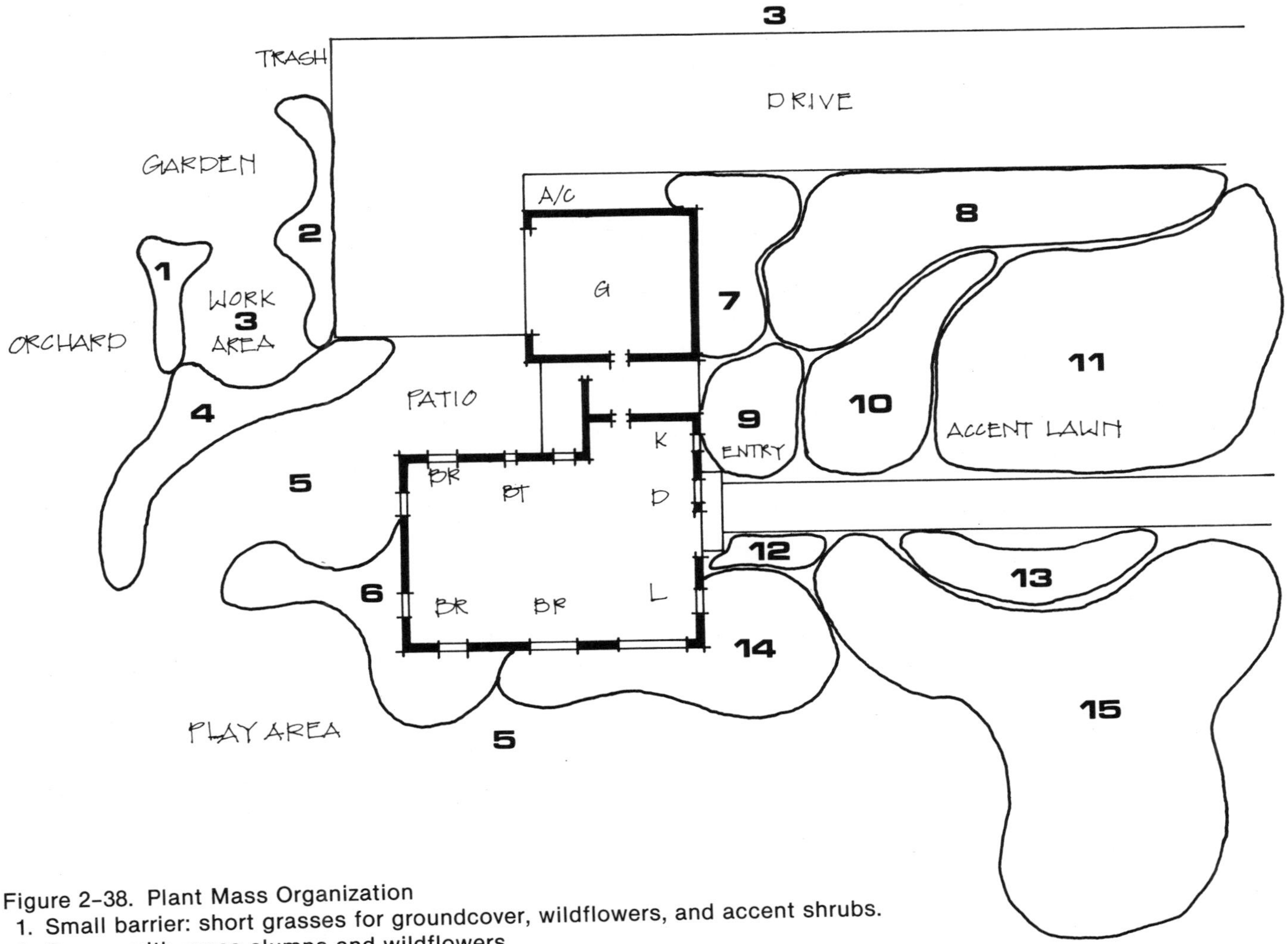

Figure 2-38. Plant Mass Organization

1. Small barrier: short grasses for groundcover, wildflowers, and accent shrubs.
2. Screen with grass clumps and wildflowers.
3. Small open space, grass.
4. Overstory/understory mix with grass ground cover and vine mix. Accent with wild flowers/grasses.
5. Lawn/open area.
6. Overstory/understory mix with small shrubs, grasses, wildflowers, and vines.
7. Shrub mass.
8. 9, 10, & 11. Lawn/open area with overmix. Accent entry.
12. & 13. Lawn area.
14. Groundcover overmix with accent for entry.
15. Lawn/open area.

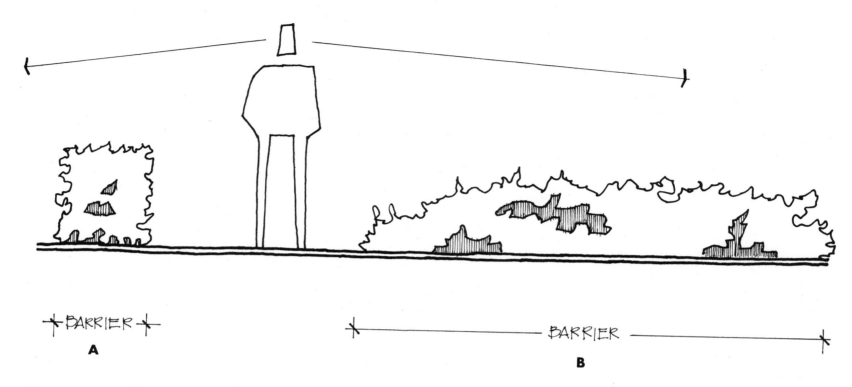

Figure 2–39. The design barrier can function more effectively if there is sufficient room in the planting arrangement. *Barrier A* may only be a small ornamental shrub mass, while *barrier B* may be composed of several shrub and grass species.

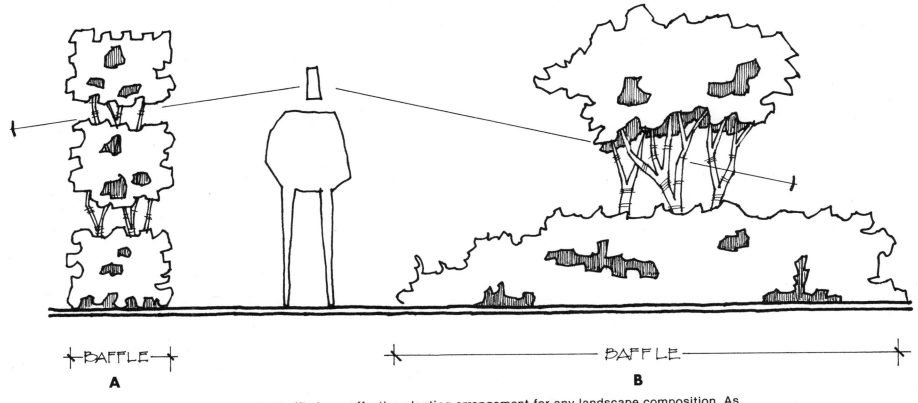

A

B

Figure 2-40. The design baffle is an effective planting arrangement for any landscape composition. As with the other architectural forms, it needs additional space to function properly.

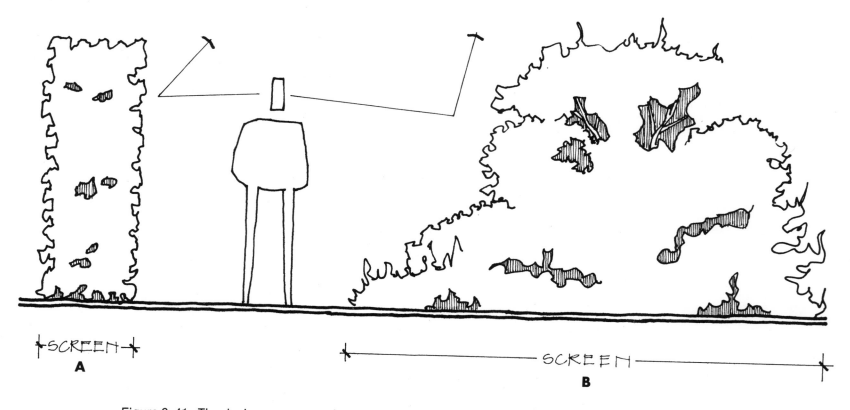

SCREEN
A

SCREEN
B

Figure 2–41. The design screen can function more effectively, too, if there is sufficient room in the planting arrangement. *Screen A* is a typical ornamental plant form requiring very little space. *Screen B*, on the other hand, will require an expanded space to function.

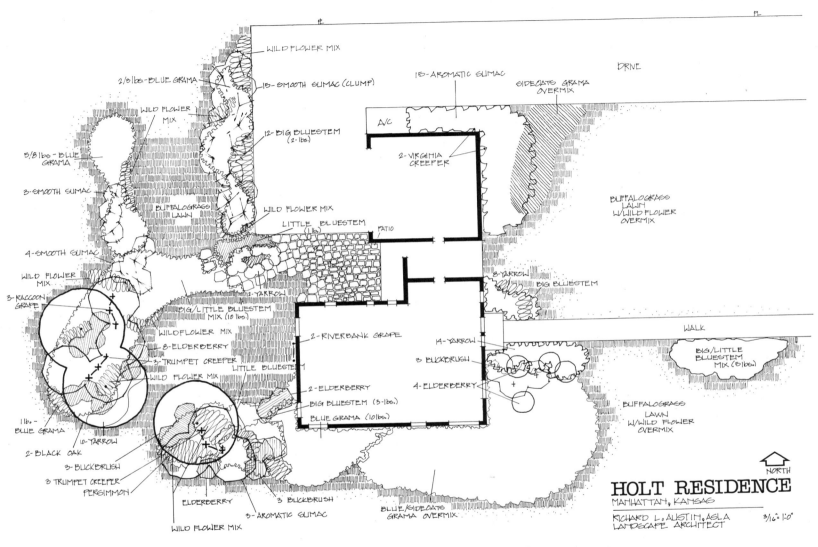

Figure 2-42. Typical residential planting plan.

Plant List

QUANT.	COMMON NAME	SCIEN. NAME	SIZE	CONDT.
TREES				
2	BLACK OAK	QUERCUS VELUTINA	4"-6" CAL.	BB
1	PERSIMMON	DIOSPYROS VIRGINIANA	4" CAL.	BB
4	STAGHORN SUMAC	RHUS TYPHINA	5'-6'	BB
18	AROMATIC SUMAC	RHUS AROMATICA	4'-5'	BR
SHRUBS AND GROUNDCOVERS				
9	BUCKBRUSH	SYMPHORICARPOS ORBICULATHS MOENCH	3'-4'	BR
15	ELDERBERRY	SAMBUCUS CANADENSIS L.	3'	BR
22	SMOOTH SUMAC	RHUS GLABRA L.	3'	BR
44	YARROW	ACHILLEA MILLEFOLIUM	CLUMPS	—
33 lbs.	WILD FLOWER MIX	VAR. #①	—	—
VINES AND GRASSES				
6	TRUMPET CREEPER	CAMSIS RADICANS	1 GAL.	—
3	RACCOON GRAPE	AMPELOPSIS CORDATA	1 GAL.	—
2	RIVERBANK GRAPE	VITIS RIPARIA	1 GAL.	—
#②	BIG BLUESTEM	ANDROPOGON GERARDI	—	
#②	LITTLE BLUESTEM	SCHIZARCHYRIUM SCOPARIUS	—	
#②	BLUE GRAMA	BOUTELOUA GRACILIS	—	
#②	SIDE OATS GRAMA	BOUTELOUA UNTIPENDULA	—	
2	VIRGINIA CREEPER	PARTHENOCISSUS QUINQUEFOLIA	1 GAL.	
#②	BUFFALOGRASS	BUCHLOE DACTYLOIDES		

NOTES:
#① SEE WILDFLOWER LIST FOR SPECIFIC SPECIES
#② SEE SPECS FOR QUANTITIES

Figure 2-43. The typical plant list.

TRANSITION

WALK

TRANSITION

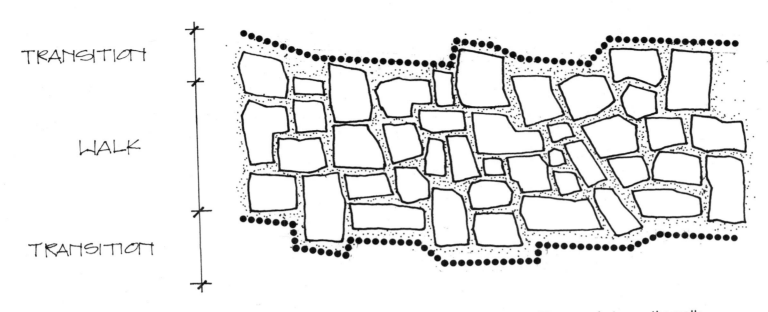

Figure 2-44. When developing a walk for the residential site, provide a transition area between the walk and adjacent planting spaces to allow for a "blending" of site elements with the natural landscape.

3. MANAGEMENT
AND IMPLEMENTATION

MANAGEMENT TECHNIQUES FOR NATURAL VEGETATION

The designer of a natural landscape composition is essentially the first manager of the project. By selecting specific design methodologies or implementation strategies for development, a long-term management program begins. The initial planting plan and the resulting management program are the final determining factor for the success or failure of the project.

From the completed planting plans, a management program can be adopted that can speed up, retard, aid, or hinder the processes that affect natural vegetation. By selectively removing certain plant species from a project site, more desirable species can be encouraged to grow and achieve design intent. The specific goals of a management program will vary with the project and with the ecological region, but are apt to include a desire for:

A diversity of plant species, including plants with showy flowers or picturesque shapes
The development of scenic vistas for on-site visitor experiences

A variety of vegetative cover, such as a combination of forest and open meadow

Management of Natural Forest Vegetation

Rarely will a designer find existing forest vegetation totally desirable for a natural landscape development. Most project areas have been lumbered, cleared for agriculture and later abandoned, or completely changed from their original conditions (Fig. 3-1).

Thinning dense stands of shrubs or young trees may be needed to accomplish the objectives of the design intent as well as the management program. Such a technique may improve the vistas, help in species diversity, and speed the growth of the more desirable plants by reducing unwanted competition.

Some thinning operations may require the use of lightly applied herbicides, with the best procedure varying with the type of herbicides, the species of vegetation, and the size of the individual plants. The selective spraying of plant foliage is rarely a good procedure. Stem application is recommended. After the removal of the undesired materials from the site, the more appropriate species from

71

Figure 3–1. This project site is marked by areas of native hardwood trees and understory shrubs as well as sections that have been severely overgrazed by livestock. The intent of the final development plan would be to provide a transitional zone of vegetation to blend the two areas together. (USDA-Soil Conservation Service)

the region may be introduced by seeding or transplanting for a more successful composition.

Management of Natural Grassland Vegetation

Natural grasslands, unlike landscaped lawns, are dominated by native grasses and many associated forbs. Vegetation within this ecological spectrum can tolerate a natural or man-made disturbance—grazing by wild herbivores and burning, for example—more easily than forest vegetation can. Fire thus becomes more important to the maintenance of a prairie in the prairie-forest transition area than in drier grasslands, but it may be a useful management tool in many grassland projects.

To maintain grasslands and prevent forest vegetation encroachment, several methods can be used. If the proj-

ect area is large and an effective fire barrier can be located at the boundaries, the cheapest method can be burning. Fire control, however, can be difficult and requires considerable equipment, trained personnel, and a knowledge of proper weather conditions.

Burning when new growth of bluestem starts in the spring is the best time to burn tall-grass or bluestem prairie in the central United States. By "best" we mean getting the greatest production out of the prairie plants. Since this occurs after certain birds have started nesting, if all the grassland is burned at that specific time each year, it will be detrimental to the nesting bird species and may be unfavorable for those that nest later because it removes cover for nesting. However, if only part of the grassland is burned in any one year, the grassland birds will nest or renest in the unburned portion, and their populations will remain satisfactory. In fact, with no burning or other selected maintenance to manage the grassland, many grassland bird and mammal species will disappear.

Mowing is effective in stopping woody plant invasion and in keeping down the accumulation of standing dead grass. Mowing once a year in midsummer—in late July—often works well. Removal of the cut forage for hay is often practiced, but when the cut grass is left in place it will compact against the soil surface, decompose rapidly, and not interfere with the development of other grassland species. If the hay is removed, the mowing should be done early enough to allow some regrowth to cover the surface before winter (Fig. 3-2).

In addition, woody plants can be kept out of grasslands by hand removal or by the use of herbicides. Herbicides should be applied only by bark or cut-stem application or by stem injection rather than by spraying. Spraying will injure or kill forbs, many of which are important contributors to the beauty of grassland projects (Fig. 3-3).

Right-of-way Management

Controlling shrubs and trees along roads and public utility lines in forested regions has been difficult. The advent of the synthetic herbicides 2,4-D and 2,4,5-T after World War II seemed to herald a solution to this problem. Public utilities and highway maintenance crews began spraying the entire length and width of many rights-of-way. The result was destruction of desirable plants and high chemical costs because the process had to be repeated periodically.

There are, therefore, three primary objectives for the right-of-way landscape:

Reduction of costs of right-of-way maintenance
Development of a relatively stable vegetation that makes tree invasion difficult

Enhancement of scenic qualities and wildlife values

These objectives may be attained by selectively killing those individual plants not desired along the easement. In the middle of high voltage, transmission line, rights-of-way, both trees and tall shrubs may be selectively removed with herbicides. After a number of years, a relatively stable vegetation will be produced, with the shrubs providing conditions in which tree growth is very poor. The selective use of herbicides is initially much cheaper than spraying the entire right-of-way and results in a much more stable vegetation. It also avoids the "brown-outs" produced by mass killing of vegetation by spraying.

REESTABLISHMENT OF NATURAL VEGETATION

Reestablishing natural vegetation can be basically easy. We are dealing with native species that, of course, are adapted to a project area. All we have to do, therefore, is let natural processes act. However, this solution is not generally acceptable because it may take from many decades to many centuries to obtain a desired state of natural vegetation. If a lack of seeds of the desired species is a problem, an obvious answer is to bring in those seeds and scatter or drill them where they are wanted.

In nature, probably less than one seed in ten thousand succeeds in producing a new plant that will live to flower because, although wild plants produce large numbers of seeds, only a few of these succeed. To duplicate the natural process, a designer would have to bring in huge quantities of seeds and repeat the planting more than once a season.

To best reestablish natural vegetation properly, knowledge of the specific area and of the particular species involved is required. However, the following principles apply in most cases.

Figure 3–2. The mowing of some native grasslands, on a project site is a management tool that can be employed to retard the development of woody vegetation. Mowed areas should be changed each year in order to maintain an improved range condition throughout the native landscape. (USDA-Soil Conservation Service)

Figure 3–3. Small areas of invading woody vegetation can be managed by the selective use of herbicides. (USDA-Soil Conservation Service)

Seedbed Preparation

Reduction in competition is essential for successful growth of a reasonable percentage of seeds. We would harvest very little corn after planting corn in an unplowed forest or grassland. Little more success is likely if we plant native materials without reducing competition from other species. Seedbed preparation procedures may vary widely, depending on the circumstances. You can plow the area if it is void of desired vegetation and soil and slope conditions permit. If desired plants are present, but other species need to be added, the preparation may be on small spots scattered over a larger area.

Species Placement

Many failures have resulted because someone saw a successful reestablishment of a species in one area and then planted that same species in another area where conditions were different. Keeping successful establishment high and costs low requires matching the location where plants are established with the places and conditions well suited to their needs.

Seed Dormancy

Cultivated plants do not have much dormancy because they have been selected to germinate promptly when placed in favorable temperature and moisture. People accustomed to working with cultivated plants often fail with wild plants because they do not realize that most wild plant seeds have an inherent dormancy. These dormancies are important in helping to time their germination to the season when they are most likely to succeed. Some are dormant because the seed coat is impervious to water or oxygen. Such seeds will not germinate in nature until decomposers (bacteria, fungi, etc.) etch the seed coat. Others have dormant embryos. In temperate climates, embryo dormancy often is removed by exposure to cold for a few weeks. There are even some seeds that must pass through two winters to completely remove the embryo dormancy. The root grows after the first cold period, after which the dormancy in the shoot is removed by the next cold period. These dormancies aid survival of the species in the wild but complicate its reseeding. To assure success with dormant seeds, each species must be treated to remove dormancies before planting if they are to germinate promptly after planting when competition is low. An alternative that may work for many species is to plant the seeds in the autumn, so that natural processes will remove dormancies and allow germination the next spring.

Obtaining Seeds of Wild Plants

Few commercial sources exist for wild plants, although there is increasing interest in and development of some commercial seed companies. The U. S. Soil Conservation Service is studying many native plants and making selections for replanting. For some you may need to actually collect the seeds from the wild. Even if you find a good natural stand, harvest of a sufficient amount of good seeds may be difficult. Sometimes seeds are unfilled or low in viability in some years, and testing for viability is complicated by dormancy. Some seeds ripen one at a time in an inflorescence, and the seeds shatter as they ripen, so that one may get only one ripe seed per inflorescence at any time. In such cases, harvest can be expensive. Not all species are as troublesome; however, do not overlook such possibilities during the planning phases.

Some success at low cost may be obtained by mowing patches of the kind of vegetation desired and scattering the cut plants over the area where they are to be reestablished. If this is repeated at several times during the year in order to get seeds that ripen at different times, a fair sample may be obtained for the project operation (Figs. 3-4 to 3-9).

MANAGING HUMAN IMPACTS

The natural landscape has become a popular and attractive alternative to the typically manicured recreation area. Interesting vegetation associations and numerous wildlife habitats can be designed to encourage more outdoor participation by a demanding public. This increased participation, however, creates additional and often hazardous impacts upon the plant communities that they would not otherwise receive.

Design of the natural landscape, when it is to be a public-use facility, should include a series of management guidelines that will help reduce potential impacts upon the vegetation. Specific methodologies should be employed to communicate, educate, interpret, and per-

suade the site visitors to protect their environments. Such methodologies might include:

1. *Heighten the awareness of the visitor* to what the recreational options are within the natural landscape project. What is offered, where, and under what circumstances may help dilute the pressures and maintain a more even balance of visitation.
2. *Control the time of the visits* by allowing the facility to become available at times and seasons when there will be less impact upon the vegetation.
3. *Limit the size of the groups* of visitors to a specific number to reduce potential stress.
4. *Limit the length of stay* on the site by individuals or groups.
5. *Limit the types of activities* for the site. Do not allow overnight camping, fires, or active recreation programs that might damage delicate vegetation.

Figure 3–4. Some seeding operations for large project sites will require mechanical applicators such as this unit attached to a small farm tractor. For planting sites of less than one acre, hand seeding may be more appropriate. (USDA-Soil Conservation Service)

Figure 3–5. This project site was planted (drilled) with seeds on 40-inch rows; the alternate rows were planted one season later. Crown growth for the larger clumps is approximately two seasons. (USDA-Soil Conservation Service)

Figure 3–6. A general view of an overseeded mix of five grass species. This stand represents plant growth of approximately three seasons. (USDA-Soil Conservation Service)

77

Figure 3–7. The final stand of grasses for this project site was reached in approximately four growing seasons. Planting methods include both mechanical seeders and hand applications. (USDA-Soil Conservation Service)

Figure 3–8. This site can be improved best by hand applications of seed mixtures to protect the soil from wind erosion and blowouts. (USDA-Soil Conservation Service)

Figure 3–9. This site may need patches of soil netting to protect the areas from wind erosion and blow-outs. (USDA-Soil Conservation Services)

APPENDIX 1
SPECIFICATIONS FOR THE PLANTING OF TREES, SHRUBS, AND VINES

GENERAL SPECIFICATIONS

1. *Description of Work*

The Landscape Contractor shall furnish all labor, equipment and materials for the planting of trees, shrubs and/or vines in accordance with these specifications. During the period of this contract, it is estimated that _____ acres will need seedbed preparation. The following species and quantity of trees, shrubs, and/or vines will be required. The material shall be planted at sites designated on the site plan or as directed by the Owner's Representative.

	Species	Spacing	Quantity Needed
Trees			
	_____	_____	_____
Shrubs	_____	_____	_____
	_____	_____	_____
Vines			
	_____	_____	_____

It is anticipated that during the period of this contract all designated acreages will be prepared and all previously listed species planted. However, the Owner shall not be obligated to the Landscape Contractor for work performance under the contract if such work is determined unnecessary or impractical by the Owner's Representative.

2. *Seedbed Preparation*

a. Area: the area requiring preplanting preparation shall include that designated portion as shown, an area of approximately _____ acres.

b. Method: a smooth firm planting area free of clods, stones, woody roots, or other foreign matter shall be prepared.

3. *Plant Material Quality*

a. All plants shall be nursery grown unless specifically authorized to be collected.

b. All trees, shrubs, and vines shall be in a good, vigorous, healthy condition, free from disease and injury. They shall be hardy under climatic conditions similar to those in the locality of the project.

c. When specified plants are not available within a reasonable distance, substitutions may be made if approved by the Owner or his/her Representative.

81

4. *Care and Handling of Plants*
   a. Plants shall be carefully handled so that roots and foliage are adequately protected from freezing, over-heating, drying out, sunscald, flooding, or other injury.
   b. Bare root plants will be placed in water or wrapped in other wet material as soon as they are unpacked at the site. Care must be taken to completely protect the roots at all times prior to planting. If not planted within two hours of unpacking, they shall be heeled-in in moist soil or organic matter in accordance with acceptable horticulture practices.
   c. Balled and burlapped plants will be protected if not planted soon after delivery by covering roots with loose soil or organic matter, such as wood shavings, pine bark, or compost. Roots shall be kept moist until planting time.
   d. Container grown plants shall have been grown in a container long enough for the root system to have developed sufficiently to hold its soil together firm and whole. No plants shall be loose in the container. If not planted soon after delivery, they shall be kept moist by frequent watering.
   e. Plants not planted immediately should be kept in a place away from direct sunlight.

5. *Planting Operations*
   a. Plant pit excavation
   (1) Tree pits shall be excavated 1 foot (30 cm) greater in diameter than the ball of earth or spread of roots and 6 inches (15 cm) deeper than the root collar.
   (2) Shrub pits shall be excavated 3 to 6 inches (7.6 cm to 15 cm) wider than the ball of earth or spread of the roots and 3 inches (7.6 cm) deeper than the root collar.
   (3) Planting holes for vines shall be sufficiently large to accommodate the roots without crowding and shall be at least as deep as the depth at which they grew in the nursery.
   (4) When hand planting with dibble (planting bar) or mattock, care shall be taken to place plants at or slightly deeper than they grew in the nursery. Plant-ing slit shall be deep enough to accommodate roots without crooks or twists. **(Figure A1–1)**
   (5) If mechanical tree planters are used, planting slit shall be deep enough to assure proper root placement. Packing wheels shall be positioned to assure no air pockets and firm placement of plant in the ground at or slightly deeper than growing position in nursery. Firming may be done with a tractor wheel or by hand.
   b. Placement of plants
   (1) Plants shall be placed in the center of the holes, plumb and straight, and at such a level that the root collar should be below the surrounding finished grade as follows:

   Trees: 3 to 6 inches (7.6 cm to 15 cm)
   Shrubs: 1 to 3 inches (2.54 cm to 7.6 cm)
   Vines: 0 to 1 inch (0 cm to 2.54 cm)

   (2) For bare root plants, spread the roots out to prevent crowding. The roots should be in approximately the same position as they were growing before trans-planting, with root collar depth as above.
   (3) All wire shall be removed from the tops and sides of burlap balls.
   (4) Container grown stock shall be removed from con-tainer with minimum damage to roots and placed at bottom of hole to assure no air pockets.
   c. Backfill
   (1) After placement of planting stock, hole shall be half filled with soil and then thoroughly watered to settle soil and exclude air pockets.
   (2) Finish filling planting hole to levels described in 5b(1) and water again. A minimum of tamping of fill may be necessary to assure that no air pockets are present.
   (3) Stock planted with a dibble or tree planter shall be firmed and irrigated by hand or with sprinkler system.
   d. Staking of trees only
   Newly planted trees need support to hold them in posi-

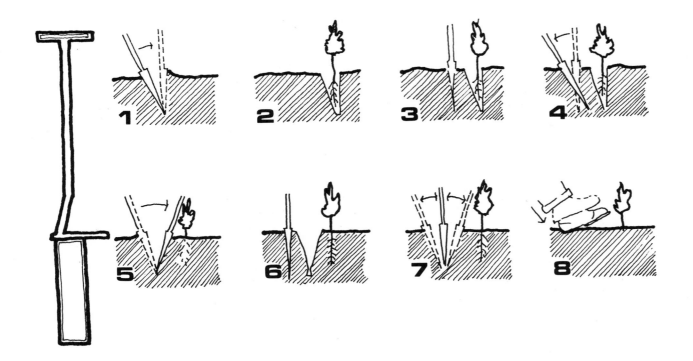

Figure A1-1. Procedures for Planting with a Dibble.
1. Insert dibble at angle shown and push forward to upright position.
2. Remove dibble and place seedling at correct depth.
3. Insert dibble 2 inches from seedling.
4. Pull handle of dibble toward plant, firming soil at bottom of roots.
5. Push handle forward, firming soil at top of roots.
6. Insert dibble 2 inches from last hole.
7. Push forward then pull backward, filling hole.
8. Fill last hole by stamping with heel.

tion and to keep the roots from loosening and the crowns from breaking. Unsupported trees often lean permanently away from prevailing winds. At planting, bracing stakes should be installed on all trees larger than 1 1/2 inch in caliper before the roots are covered. The stakes should be strong enough to hold the trunk rigidly in place. Place the stakes 3 to 18 inches (7.6 cm to 45.72 cm) from the trunk before the planting hole is filled. Fasten the trunk to the stakes with canvas tape or loops of wire passed through a section of rubber or plastic hose or similar soft material. Bare wire will scrape or cut the bark. (Figure A1–3)

e. Pruning and mulching
  (1) If not prepruned, bare root trees and shrubs should be pruned after planting to increase survival probabilities and preserve the natural character of the plants. One-fourth to one-third of the top shall be removed. Pine trees shall not be top pruned. Cuts over 1 inch (2.54 cm) in diameter shall be painted with an approved tree paint.
  (2) Immediately after planting operations are completed, all tree and shrub pits shall be covered with a 2-inch (5.08 cm) layer of an acceptable mulch, such as hay, pine bark, wood shavings, or other porous material.

f. Fertilization
  Fertilization is required as per Designer's recommendations during this operation.

6. *Time of Planting*
The following planting dates are recommended (times will vary with geographic regions):
a. Optimum time
  Bare root stock: December 1 to March 1
  Balled and burlapped: December 1 to March 1
  Container grown: December 1 to March 1
b. Maximum time
  Bare root stock: November 15 to April 1
  Balled and burlapped: November 15 to April 15
  Container grown: can be planted during most seasons of the year

7. *Equipment for Planting*
The equipment that is recommended to meet the above specifications and to complete the work in the time allotted is as follows:
One to one and a half ton stake body truck for hauling of materials.
One to two ton stake body with winch. Winch shall be mechanically operated and with the drum mounted behind the cab equipped with a minimum of 100 feet (30.5 cm) of 1/2-inch winch line (flexible cable). All tractors and equipment used on the slopes for all operations will be held with this truck and winch line as directed by the Government Representative or his Designee.
Two farm-type tractors, four wheel, low center of gravity, minimum H.P. of 45 on the drawbar.
One tandem disk plow, heavy duty, with three-point hookup.
One tillage tool, chisel type, with three-point hookup.
One water truck or tank on trailer with hose and pump.
One soil auger, three-point hookup.
All equipment must be in good repair and operating condition. When working on slopes, all equipment will be held with truck and winch lines as directed by the Owner's Representative.

8. *Payments*
All work performed under the contract will be paid for at the unit price bid "per acre" for seedbed preparation and bid "per unit" for plant material. Determination of acreages and units during any estimate period as well as the final acreage and units will be made by the Owner's Representative.

9. *Protection After Planting*
If the Designer/Owner's Representative determines that plantings should be protected from grazing by domestic livestock, a permanent fence shall be constructed around the site to exclude such livestock.

10. *Damages—Repairs*
The Landscape Contractor will be required to repair all damages to slopes, fences, etc., caused by his/her operations under the contract. Damages due to weather or

Figure A1-2. Protect above-ground irrigation equipment from construction equipment, planting operations, and large wildlife or livestock abuse. It is important that these instruments remain intact during the critical planting program.

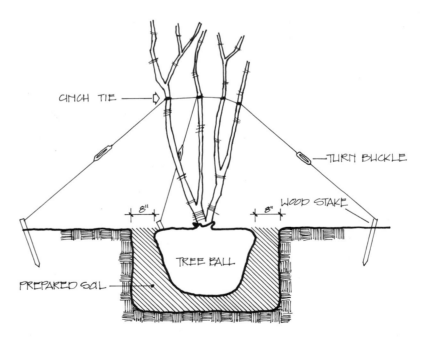

Figure A1-3.

causes beyond the control and without the fault or negligence of the Landscape Contractor will not be the responsibility of the Landscape Contractor.

SEEDLING TREE PLANTING

In order to establish or reinforce a stand of trees that would conserve soil or site moisture, the following specifications may apply.

1. *Spacing*

   Tree spacing is related to the purpose of the planting, the site, and the size of maintenance equipment. Suggested spacings are as follows:

Spacing (Feet)	Square Feet (Per Tree)	Number of Trees Per Acre
2 × 2 (0.6m × 0.6m)	4	10,890
5 × 5 (1.52m × 1.52m)	25	1,742
6 × 6 (1.83m × 1.83m)	36	1,210
6 × 8 (1.83m × 2.44m)	48	907
8 × 8 (2.44m × 2.44m)	64	680
10 × 14 (3.05m × 4.27m)	140	311
12 × 12 (3.66m × 3.66m)	144	302
12 × 16 (3.66m × 4.88m)	192	227
14 × 14 (4.27m × 4.27m)	196	222
10 × 20 (3.05m × 6.1m)	200	218

2. *Planting Stock*

   (This guide is to be used as a reference when advising clients as to the size and quality of nursery stock desirable for use in tree plantings. Larger stock or containerized stock is also acceptable for use. All undersized, poorly rooted, diseased, or otherwise poor quality trees should be disposed of.)
   a. Broadleaf species
      Seedlings not less than 7/32 inch or more than 3/8 inch

in caliper 1 inch above the root collar are recommended. Planting stock offered by most commercial nurseries in the 18-inch to 24-inch size meet this standard.
   b. Coniferour species
      Planting stock must have a good balance between top and root. Seedlings should be two to three years old and 5 inches to 12 inches tall. Seedlings should be either transplants or bed root pruned.
   c. Greenhouse materials
      Container-grown seedlings that meet the size requirements above are adequate for field planting.

3. *Handling and Storage*
   a. Trees received from the nursery are normally stored by the Landscape Contractor or by the Owner until they can be planted. Storage may be cold storage, cellar-type storage, or heeling-in.
   b. During all stages of handling and storage, the tops of the plants should be kept dry and free of mold. The roots will be kept moist and cool. Plants that have been allowed to dry, to heat in the bale, and/or to develop mold will not be planted.
   c. Damaged stock will be culled.

4. *Planting Methods*

   Trees may be planted by hand, machine, or direct seeding. Various hand tools and machines are available for seedling planting, most of which are suitable if used properly.

5. *Time of Planting*
   a. Plant only when the ground is frost free. Trees and shrubs should not be planted when the temperature is freezing or below.
   b. During planting operations, roots of trees or shrubs should be protected from drying out. Avoid planting on hot, windy days.
   c. Soil around trees and shrubs must be packed firmly enough to eliminate all air pockets.
   d. The planting trench or pocket must be deep and wide enough to permit the roots to be spread out as naturally as possible.
   e. Trees and shrubs shall be planted in a nearly vertical

position, with the root collars approximately 1 inch below the soil surface.

f. Only dormant seedlings should be planted.

g. Hay or straw mulches should not be used. If a mulch is desired, use clean corn cobs or wood chips.

6. *Replanting*

Trees that fail to survive should be replaced for the first two years following planting. Generally the same species that was originally planted should be used.

7. *Control of Competitive Vegetation*

Competitive vegetation shall be controlled for a minimum of three years after the date of planting. On those sites where severe wind erosion is a hazard and trees have been planted in shallow furrows, competitive vegetation shall be controlled by the following alternative methods:

a. Mow between the rows to keep vegetation in check. Mow approximately once each month during the growing season.

b. Rototill a 12- to 24-inch strip, 2 to 4 inches deep, along each side of the row approximately once each month during the growing season.

c. Hand hoe or weed around each tree.

8. *Protection*

a. Livestock shall be excluded from the planting area.

b. The planting shall be protected from fire. Maintain breaks and isolation strips.

c. Protect trees from wild animal damage.

d. Mice, gophers, and other rodents may be controlled by poison baits. Gopher baits are best placed with "gopher-getter" type machines. (*If you use pesticides, apply them only when needed and handle with care. Follow the directions and heed all precautions on the container label. If pesticides are not handled or applied properly, they may be injurious to humans, animals, fish, and insects and may contaminate water supplies.*)

e. Check for insect and disease damage by regular inspections. Seek professional assistance for diagnosis and control measures.

APPENDIX 2
DESIGN CRITERIA AND TECHNICAL SPECIFICATIONS FOR THE DEVELOPMENT OF WATER FEATURES

SPRING DESIGN AND DEVELOPMENT

Site Selection

In determining the suitability of a site for development, consideration should be given to the need for and feasibility of protection from flooding, silting, and contamination. An effort should be made to measure the flow of any existing springs to aid in making a determination as to whether or not flow after development will meet project requirements. An investigation of site conditions, including borings, should be made to provide information for use in planning and development. There are four general types of springs:

Perched or contact spring
Stream depression spring
Cavernous (fracture) rock spring
Artesian spring

Development

In general, the development of a spring involves (a) cleanout and construction of a collecting system, and (b) construction of a sump or spring box. As springs do not occur in any fixed patterns, many types of developments are used.

1. *Perched or contact spring.* This type of spring generally occurs where an impermeable layer outcrops beneath a water-bearing permeable layer. These springs should be developed by intercepting and collecting the flow from the water-bearing formation. Collection trenches are normally used.
2. *Stream depression spring.* This common type of spring often occurs on the bank of a stream or drainageway where the channel has cut into a permeable water-bearing stratum underlain by an impermeable layer. The outlet of the spring is below the elevation of the water table in the permeable layer. To develop this type of spring, a clean-

out is almost always required. If water issues from a single opening, a collection system will not be required, but an enlargement of the opening and a spring box or sump will probably be needed.

3. *Cavernous (fracture) rock spring.* This type of spring is associated with cavernous rock. It normally occurs where rock is exposed in the abutment of a drainageway and most frequently at the point of contact between the rock stratum and an impervious underlying layer. The development usually consists of cleaning out fractures and enlargement as needed, together with collection of the flow and conveyance to a sump or box.

4. *Artesian spring.* This type of spring normally occurs at a fissure or break in an impervious stratum, with the water source being an underlying pervious water-bearing layer so positioned that the water table is always above the outlet point of the spring. Development usually consists of removing obstructions, cleaning, enlarging, or lowering the outlet elevation. Sumps or spring boxes may also be used.

PONDS AND SMALL LAKES

For developing or improving impounded water to produce fish for domestic use or recreation, to improve favorable water habitat, and to supplement natural food supplies, the following are minimum qualifications for the design of these types of features:

1. Failure of the structure would not result in loss of life; in damage to homes, commercial or industrial buildings, main highways, or railroads; or in interruption of the use or service of public utilities.

2. The product of the storage times the effective height of the dam does not exceed 3,000. Storage is defined as the volume (acre-feet) in the reservoir below the elevation of the crest of the emergency spillway. Effective height of the dam is defined as the difference in elevation (feet) between the emergency spillway crest and the lowest point

in the cross section taken along the centerline of the dam.

3. The vertical distance between the lowest point along the centerline of the dam and the crest of the emergency spillway does not exceed 35 feet (10.67m).

Planning Considerations

1. Select a site that has sufficient, but not excessive, drainage area and is surrounded by vegetation (grass).

2. Locate the dam in an area that will provide the greatest depth with the least amount of fill.

3. Sites should be located in areas where seepage is not a problem.

4. The land adjacent to the pond can be developed into a desirable wildlife area by proper seeding of grasses or the planting of suitable trees and shrubs.

5. Locate development in an area that will save the greatest number of trees and natural vegetation.

Pond Size, Depth, and Water Quality

1. The minimum size for warm-water runoff ponds is one-half acre. Spring-fed ponds for trout are one-quarter acre. Minimum depth for runoff ponds is 10 feet (3.05m) and for spring-fed ponds, 6 to 8 (1.83m to 2.44m) feet over at least one-quarter of the pond area.

2. The drainage area into the fish pond should not include potential sources of pollution. That is, ponds should not be located below feedlots or areas where land treatment does not restrict the movement of pesticides and fertilizers or sediment into the pond. Using the palm of the hand as a measuring device for visibility, ponds with visibility into the water of less than 4 inches (10.16cm) because of suspended sediment are not recommended for stocking. Ponds with visibility into the water of from 4 to 10 inches (10.16 cm to 25.4 cm) because of suspended sediment are recommended for stocking with catfish only. Ponds with visibility in the water of over 10 (25.4cm) inches are suitable for other kinds of fish.

APPENDIX 3
SPECIFICATIONS FOR THE PLANTING OF CRITICAL AREAS

Stabilizing Critical Areas by Planting Grass

1. *Site Preparation*
   Necessary shaping and smoothing shall be made before seedbed preparations are started. On steep gully banks, earth-moving machinery should be used to shape the area in a manner that seedbed preparation and seeding operations can be carried out.

2. *Seedbed Preparation*
   Critical areas are usually low in fertility and present difficult problems in establishing permanent cover. Seeding of grasses may be made according to the *tilled seedbed* method. Provide for or have available a seedbed firm and compact beneath and loose and open on the surface to at least a 2-inch (5.08cm) depth. This is necessary to permit anchoring mulch. Plant the grass seed and immediately apply and anchor a mulch cover. Preferred mulching material is native hay. It must be relatively free of weeds.

3. *Grass Seeding*
   a. Method of seeding grass
      A grass drill is preferred. The drill should be equipped with double-disk openers, depth bands, press wheels or drag chains, and seed boxes with separate boxes or drivers for each seed tube that will handle both chaffy and free-flowing seeds. On areas too steep for equipment operation, seed mixtures may be broadcast. When seed is broadcast and not covered, double the rate of seeding. Cover seed if possible.

   b. Hydroseeding
      A mixture of seed, fertilizer, and mulch materials should be used. Limit the application to 150 pounds of solids per 100 gallons of water. If a legume seed is in the mixture, apply lime and fertilizer first.

   c. Seeding dates
      (1) Cool-season mixtures: August 15 to April 30
      (2) Warm-season mixtures: October 1 to June 15

   d. Grasses to plant for permanent and intermediate duration
      (1) Mixtures planted will provide a minimum of 60 P.L.S. seeds per square foot.
      (2) Mixtures for permanent planting will contain a mixture of two or more species. A single species may be more practical on some residential or recreational areas.

4. *Fertilizing*

On sites that are low in fertility, use 10 to 30 pounds each of nitrogen and phosphorous per acre.

5. *Irrigation*

Where water and an irrigation system are available, apply in small, frequent amounts until plants are established.

6. *Maintenance and Protection*
   a. Critical areas need all the vegetative cover that is possible to reduce soil erosion. Livestock of any kind should not have access to the areas during the growing season.
   b. Infestation of grasshoppers should be sprayed for control when necessary during the establishment of vegetation.
   c. Control fires.

Stabilizing Critical Areas by Sodding or Sprigging

Obtain seedlings, plants, crowns, or sod plugs that are healthy and have received proper care in lifting from the nursery and transporting to the site. Planting material should never be allowed to become dry or overheated due to improper packing and hauling. Keep plant materials moist and as cool as possible after delivery to the site until they are set.

1. *Site Preparation*

The surface to be sodded or sprigged shall be reasonably smooth, even, and free from debris. The surface shall be brought to the correct alignment, grade, and cross section.

2. *Sodding*

The sod should be in strips or blocks of a native grass mixture. Sod materials are to be taken from good, solid thick-growing stands. Sod shall be cut in strips of uniform width and to a uniform thickness of at least 3 inches for tall grass and 1/2 to 1 1/2 inches for short grasses. Lay sod within 24 hours from the time it is cut. Sod strips shall be carefully placed in rows across (at right angles to) the direction of slope. The sod strips shall be placed together tightly so that no open joints are left between strips or between the ends of strips. Any spaces between joints shall be filled with topsoil and all edges of sod covered with topsoil at least 2 inches (5.08cm) in depth. The edge of the sod at the top of slopes shall be turned slightly under and a layer of soil compacted over the edge so as to conduct surface water over and onto the top of the sod. On slopes steeper than three horizontal to one vertical or where high velocity flows are likely to occur over newly sodded areas, the strips should be held in place by wooden pegs or anchored with jute netting or other commercial netting over the sod.

3. *Planting or Sodding Dates*
   a. Cool-season vegetation: August 1 to October 15
      March 1 to May 30
   b. Warm-season vegetation: March 1 to May 30

4. *Fertilizing*

Fertilizer shall be applied before the sod is placed or sprigs are planted. On sites that are low in fertility, cut slopes, or areas with little or no surface soil, use 10 to 30 pounds each of nitrogen and phosphorous per acre.

5. *Irrigation*

Water when necessary during the first growing season to insure survival of sods.

Stabilizing Critical Areas by Planting Shrubs and Trees

1. *Site Preparation*

Soil preparation prior to planting is essential to survival of a woody planting. Elimination of competing vegetation and conservation of soil moisture are accomplished by good site preparation.

2. *Tree and Shrub Planting*
   a. Plant only high-quality, vigorous specimens.
   b. Plant in the early spring months for optimum soil moisture and favorable temperatures to start growth.
   c. Use a planting bar, shovel, or tree planter.
   d. Apply irrigation water, if available, to increase survival and growth rate.
   e. Reduce competing vegetation when excessive. Protect the vegetation area from grazing, wild fires, and rodents.

APPENDIX 4
STANDARDS AND SPECIFICATIONS FOR THE DEVELOPMENT OF WILDLIFE HABITATS

The Upland Habitat

The upland habitat can be created or improved for various wildlife species by planting of food and/or cover plants.

1. *Quail, Dove, and Songbirds*
   a. Food plants (where native)

Annuals	Reseeding Annuals	Perennials
Grain sorghum	Browntop millet	Kliengrass
Oats	Sesame	Bicolor lespedeza
Cowpeas	Vetch	Sericea lespedeza
Corn	Reseeding soybeans	Blue panicum
	Partridgepea	Bahiagrass

   b. Cover plants
      Select species of perennial grasses or woody plants adapted to the site and local conditions.

c. Size of plantings
   Food plantings should cover 1/2 to 3 acres per planting or one planting for each 25 to 35 acres. It is desirable for quail food plantings to be made near low-growing shrub cover. Cover plantings should be in clumps of ten or more plants, one for each 25 to 35 acres.

2. *Deer and Turkey*
   a. Food plants (where native)

Annuals	Reseeding Annuals	Perennials
Oats	Clovers	Blue panicum
Rye	Vetch	Honeysuckle
Wheat	Singletary peas	Fescue
Corn	Partridgepea	Kudzu
Cowpeas		
Grain sorghum		

93

b. Size of plantings

Between 1 and 2 acres should be planted if only turkey are in the area, 2 to 10 acres, if deer are already present. One planting for each 75 to 100 acres.

Wetland Habitat

Creating or improving the natural landscape for ducks and geese, fur-bearing animals, or other wildlife species should be as follows:

1. *Woodland Duck Ponds*

Construct an embankment with a water control structure to flood and drain hardwood bottoms for duck management. Flood the bottoms with water 4 to 15 inches deep over 80 percent of the area from approximately October to March to create mast. Drain the pond from March to October so the trees will not be killed. If the entire flooded area has a dense tree canopy, one or more openings should be cleared to make the area accessible to the ducks and geese.

2. *Openland Duck Ponds*

Plant food materials as required for the location and construct an embankment where needed to permit flooding with 4 to 15 inches of water from October to March. Plant water-tolerant shrubs or tall grasses along the edges for concealment.

3. *Marshes*

To improve the marsh habitat install water-control structures or small embankments to hold shallow water or existing natural marshes where necessary. Manage the water level of the marsh to permit spring drying and fall and winter flooding to produce native duck foods.

APPENDIX 5
CASE STUDIES

The following case studies are presented to illustrate design by professional landscape architectural firms and to provide examples of current state-of-the-art methodologies. The first is the Veterans Administration National Cemetery in Fort Custer, Michigan, designed by Johnson, Johnson, and Roy, Inc. of Ann Arbor, Michigan. The second is an example of the mixture of natural and ornamental plant species for Taylor University in Upland, Indiana, designed by LeRoy Troyer and Associates of Mishawaka, Indiana.

VETERANS ADMINISTRATION NATIONAL CEMETERY*

Landscape Character

Landscape development for the cemetery has carefully considered the retention of the natural setting, not the creation and maintenance of a manicured landscape.

Visitors will notice that care has been taken to conserve existing natural areas, woodlots, slopes, and wetlands. Where construction of roads, buildings, and burial sections has disturbed natural areas, trees, shrubs, and groundcover native to this area have been used to revegetate disturbed areas. Native plants have been used to reforest some areas formerly

*This excerpt is reprinted by permission of Johnson, Johnson, and Roy, Inc.

cleared for farm fields and to ensure privacy within the cemetery by screening adjacent public roads.

Consistent with energy conservation needs and environmental responsibility is the necessity to understand techniques for maintaining the native landscape. The existing sandy loam soil in some areas of the cemetery is thin and impoverished. Any disturbance to the soil cover could result in permanent scars unless the soil were enriched and replanted. Plants and grass mixtures indigenous to this site are used in burial sections and in replanted areas since they will require minimal care.

A sensitive planting program responds to these qualities, seeking to reinforce the plant community, modify it by introducing alternative species, or eradicate it and establish a new community. Which of these alternatives is pursued depends not only on the quality of the community but also on the treatment of the land unit in accordance with the Master Plan.

Design Criteria

Considerations of conservation and maintenance of the natural landscape led to the design criteria discussed in this section.

1. *Preservation.* The quality of existing plant communities is reinforced through the removal of invader species, scrub undergrowth, and diseased and damaged specimens. Ex-

tending these efforts into projected phase development helps to keep future maintenance costs low by preventing growth of undesirable species.

2. *Reforestation.* Areas that are cleared during construction are replanted to encourage plant associations that develop naturally under those specific site conditions.

3. *Transition.* Plantings soften the edge between developed and natural sectors. Such plantings unify these areas as well as provide a protective buffer where the woodland edge has been cleared.

4. *Definition of spaces.* Spaces for different functions are enclosed by plantings to define the space. Extensions of the existing wooded areas provide smaller spaces of a more intimate scale.

5. *Views.* Plantings direct views by framing interesting and attractive features such as ponds, kettleholes, or the flagpole display area. Visual screens of plant materials serve to close off undesired views to perimeter public roads.

6. *Energy Conservation.* Vegetation is implemented as an energy conservation measure, providing buildings with a protective wind buffer during the winter and shade in the summer. Snow accumulation is controlled through the use of wind channels formed by planting masses.

7. *Accent.* In areas of special interest and in pedestrian zones, plantings provide color, texture, and form to highlight and emphasize the special character of these places.

8. *Visual Direction.* Landmark plantings of notable height, mass, and contrast assist visitors in movement on the site.

9. *Existing Character of the Site.* Open fields or former farms with a variety of fieldstone, and prominent woodland with gently sloping terrain suggest a palette of material that closely relates to these natural settings.

Site Guidelines

Alternative building materials and construction techniques which could be used to achieve a natural parklike environment were investigated.

The resulting vocabulary of designed elements is a "family" of materials and details that meet the following criteria:

1. *Appropriateness.* The element fits into the cemetery's environment and is both inviting and functional.

2. *Compatibility.* It is expressive of natural and native material.

3. *Flexibility.* It is able to adapt to future expansion needs and programs.

4. *Continuity.* Common materials theme with interrelated forms and colors.

5. *Maintenance.* This is reasonable but the cost is realistic and has ease of accomplishment.

Land Management

The land management plan for the cemetery reflects a need to conserve energy and an awareness of the natural resources of the site. Because most of the soils on the site are limited in their capacity to support grasses and other plant materials, most developable land requires some sort of soil improvement before planting. The bulk of the areas designated for development requires some clearing of vegetation. Following clearing, a final evaluation of soil conditions is made to determine the type and amount of remedial work necessary to prepare the soil for development and landscaping.

Successful land management includes enriching the soil in certain areas with inexpensive, readily available organic, nutrient-rich humus in combination with nitrogen-fixing cover crops. These techniques improve the fertility and moisture retention capacity of the native sandy soils so as to provide water for turf grasses during dry spells.

The primary aim is to build the topsoil up substantially prior to development under a management program that does not include permanent, automated, underground irrigation. Because of the sandy and gravelly nature of the site, soil moisture retention capacities are very low and therefore soils are prone to severe drought in June, July, and August of most years. Marked improvement of this condition is necessary to maintain turf in certain areas. Accordingly, it is necessary to increase the soil moisture retention capacity and create a soil environment conducive to long-term maintenance of grasses. A portable sprinkler system is used to establish lawn areas, since a permanent underground system would be inconsistent with the concept of life cycle costs, energy conservation, and the establishment of a native landscape character. In the drier periods of summer, grass areas may "brown-out" but the drought resistant grasses will recover and become green again following late summer and early fall rains.

A management program of woodlots includes the selective cutting of undesirable trees and the replanting with more desirable species or merely allowing more light in to allow competing trees to flourish.

Major reforestation is achieved with an eye to the future; tree seedlings are planted at relatively low cost in masses or drifts. In time, these trees will grow into significant stands of trees for the enjoyment of future generations of visitors.

The Committal Service Shelter

The Committal Service Shelters are located adjacent to the Wetland Corridor in a mature oak and hickory grove. This unique area was chosen for its quiet atmosphere, full canopy trees, and outstanding vistas out over the pond and marsh. This attractive setting will leave a lasting impression on families, friends, and other visitors.

The shelter sites are situated off the primary road on a one-way loop drive with a pull-off lane for ten cars at each shelter. Existing native plant material between shelters is retained to ensure privacy. The shelters are oriented for maximum protection from inclement weather and take full advantage of surrounding views.

The shelter's simple shed roof and warm-tone materials are in character with the cemetery's architectural theme established in the Administrative Building and in harmony with the surrounding environment (Figs. A5-1 to A5-5).

TAYLOR UNIVERSITY*

The visual qualities and landscape values are all part of the Master Plan. This section will address these various issues, along with the generation of a Master Landscape Planting Plan.

1. *Visual Image.* The visual impact of the landscape has various effects on different people. But it has been proven that visual effects do set the mood of the person's activities for most of that day. It is for this reason that it is so important to consider the visual quality in the short-range and long-range planning.

The campus, as it is now, is lacking a major visual focus; however, with proper placement of facilities, a major focus could be created. As has been stated before, the campus has various site dynamics that can be related to various site or visual axis lines. These axis lines all appear to converge at one particular point on the central campus. At this point, it would seem essential to have some kind of focal point that the entire campus could be "drawn to" and have a visual relationship with. This focal point may be a sculpture, bell tower, or even a specimen of landscape material.

As has been done in the past at Taylor University, as construction and site development expand, burial of overhead wire lines would improve the visual image. New utilities should be placed, when possible, in common utility trenches or tunnels. This will allow ease of maintenance, repairs, and installation of future energy and communication lines.

The University's visual image could also be impacted by the use of landscape plantings. Areas that have high priority for visual impact would include major entrances, building entrances, "people places," etc.

One method of unifying the visual qualities of the campus would be to use unified materials throughout the campus, i.e., building materials, paving surfaces, landscape plantings, etc., as has been done in the past at Taylor. There exist some walkways that have an asphalt paving over areas with concrete. Improvement of these areas to one unified material type will unify these visual qualities.

*This excerpt is reprinted by permission of LeRoy Troyer and Associates.

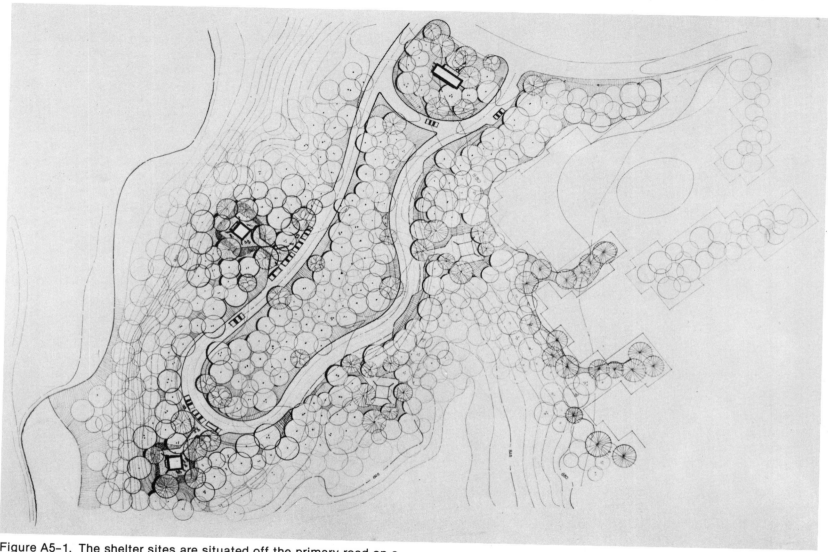

Figure A5–1. The shelter sites are situated off the primary road on a oneway loop drive with a pull-off lane for ten cars at each shelter.

Figure A5–2. The shelters are oriented for maximum protection from inclement weather and take full advantage of surrounding views.

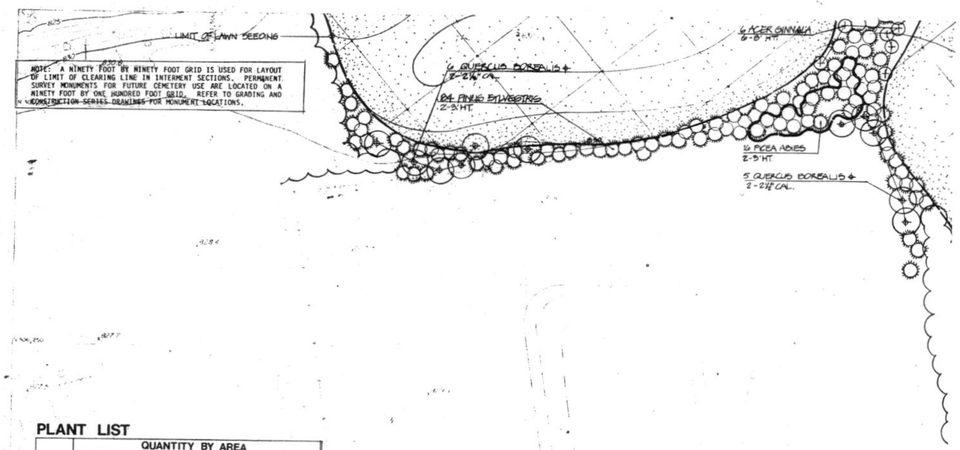
LIMIT OF LAWN SEEDING
NOTE: A NINETY FOOT BY NINETY FOOT GRID IS USED FOR LAYOUT OF LIMIT OF CLEARING LINE IN INTERMENT SECTIONS. PERMANENT SURVEY MONUMENTS FOR FUTURE CEMETERY USE ARE LOCATED ON A NINETY FOOT BY ONE HUNDRED FOOT GRID. REFER TO GRADING AND CONSTRUCTION SERIES DRAWINGS FOR MONUMENT LOCATIONS.
6 QUERCUS BOREALIS
2-2½" CAL.
84 PINUS SYLVESTRIS
2-3' HT.
6 ACER GINNALA
6-8' HT.
16 PICEA ABIES
2-3' HT.
5 QUERCUS BOREALIS
2-2½" CAL.

PLANT LIST

	TOTAL QTY.	ADM BLDG (L-50)	COM SHR (L-51)	SERV FAC (L-51)	1 (L-43)	2 (L-44)	3 (L-45)	4 (L-46)	5 (L-47)	6 (L-48)	7 (L-49)	SCIENTIFIC NAME	COMMON NAME	SIZE	ROOT	REMARKS
		QUANTITY BY AREA — SEE SHEET NUMBER														
CANOPY TREES	17				5		12					ACER RUBRUM	RED MAPLE	2"-2½" CAL.	B-B	5'-6' BRANCHING HEIGHT
	71						52	19				QUERCUS ALBA	WHITE OAK	2"-2½" CAL.	B-B	5'-6' BRANCHING HEIGHT
	248				26	22	101	68		31		QUERCUS BOREALIS	RED OAK	2"-2½" CAL.	B-B	5'-6' BRANCHING HEIGHT
	18	7						8				QUERCUS BOREALIS	RED OAK	3-3½" CAL.	B-B	6-8' BRANCHING HEIGHT
	97				4	11	18	49		15		QUERCUS COCCINEA	SCARLET OAK	2"-2½" CAL.	B-B	5'-6' BRANCHING HEIGHT
	56	3				13		33				QUERCUS COCCINEA	SCARLET OAK	3-3½" CAL.	B-B	6-8' BRANCHING HEIGHT, SPEC.
	9	9										FRAXINUS LANCEOLATA 'MARSHALL'S'	MARSHALL'S SEEDLESS ASH	3'-3½" CAL.	B-B	6-8' BRANCHING HEIGHT, SPEC.
EVERGREEN TREES	109	48		3	20	38						PINUS RESINOSA	RED PINE	6-8' HT.	B-B	FULL, HEAVY, UNSHEARED
	45					45						PINUS RESINOSA	RED PINE	4-5' HT.	B-B	FULL, HEAVY, UNSHEARED
	260				260							PINUS RESINOSA	RED PINE	2-3' HT.	B-B	
	92				59		33					PINUS STROBUS	WHITE PINE	2-3' HT.	B-B	FULL, HEAVY, UNSHEARED
	164				155		9					PINUS SYLVESTRIS	SCOTS PINE	2'-3' HT.	B-B	
	43				3	40						PINUS SYLVESTRIS	SCOTS PINE	6-8' HT.	B-B	FULL, HEAVY, UNSHEARED
	38					38						PICEA ABIES	NORWAY SPRUCE	6'-8' HT.	B-B	FULL, HEAVY, UNSHEARED
	110				110							PICEA ABIES	NORWAY SPRUCE	2-3' HT.	B-B	
SMALL/FLOWERING TREES	11				6		5					ACER GINNALA	AMUR MAPLE	6-8' HT.	B-B	MULTI-STEM
	25		8						14		3	AMELANCHIER GRANDIFLORA	SERVICEBERRY	6'-8' HT.	B-B	MULTI-STEM
	4	4										CERCIS CANADENSIS ALBA	WHITEBUD	2½"-3" CAL.	B-B	TREE FORM, MATCHED HVY. SPEC.
	11								11			CORNUS ALTERNIFOLIA	PAGODA DOGWOOD	6'-8' HT	B-B	MULTI-STEM
	10		10									CORNUS FLORIDA	WHITE FLOWERING DOGWOOD	2½"-3" CAL.	B-B	SINGLE STEM, FULL CROWNS
	34				11	13	12					CRATAEGUS CRUS-GALLI	COCKSPUR HAWTHORNE	6'-8' HT	B-B	MULTI-STEM
	38	20				18						CRATAEGUS PHAENOPYRUM	WASHINGTON HAWTHORNE	2"-2½" CAL.	B-B	SINGLE STEM, BR. HT. 3', MATCHED, FULL
	6				6							CRATAEGUS PHAENOPYRUM	WASHINGTON HAWTHORNE	10'-12' HT.	B-B	MULTI-STEM, FULL CROWNS
	31			7	17	10						MALUS FLORIBUNDA	JAPANESE FLOWERING CRAB	2"-2½" CAL.	B-B	SINGLE STEM, FULL CROWNS
DECIDUOUS SHRUBS	60		60									ARONIA MELANOCARPA	BLACK CHOKEBERRY	2'-3' HT.	BR	MIN. 3 CANES, 2'+
	42			42								CHAENOMELES JAPONICA	JAPANESE FLOWERING QUINCE	18"-24" HT.	B-B	MIN. 5 CANES, 18"+
	150				150							CORNUS RACEMOSA	GRAY DOGWOOD	3'-4' HT.	BR	MIN 5 CANES, 3'+
	12	12										ILEX VERTICILLATA NANA	DWARF WINTERBERRY	18"-24" HT.	BR	MIN. 5 CANES, 18"+
	690								490		200	RHUS AROMATICA	FRAGRANT SUMAC	2'-3' HT.	BR	MIN. 6 CANES, 2'+
	32	32										RHUS AROMATICA 'LO-GROW'	LO-GROW FRAGRANT SUMAC	18"-24" HT.	BR	MIN. 5 CANES, 18"+
	40				40							RHUS GLABRA	SMOOTH SUMAC	3'-4' HT.	BR	MIN. 4 CANES, 3'+
	59					40					19	VIBURNUM DENTATUM	ARROWWOOD VIBURNUM	4'-5' HT.	B-B	MIN. 5 CANES, 4'+
	22			22								VIBURNUM SIEBOLDII	SIEBOLD VIBURNUM	4'-5' HT.	B-B	MIN. 5 CANES, 4'+
	7	4		3								VIBURNUM TOMENTOSUM MARIESI	MARIES DOUBLEFILE VIBURNUM	3'-4' HT.	B-B	FULL SPECIMENS, UNIFORM
	35	35										VIBURNUM TRILOBUM COMPACTUM	DWARF CRANBERRY BUSH	24"-30" HT.	B-B	UNIFORM, FULL SPECIMENS
EVERGREEN SHRUBS	262	262										JUNIPERUS SABINA 'BROADMOOR'	BROADMOOR JUNIPER	15"-18" SPR.	BB/CONT	UNIFORM
	74		74									TAXUS CANADENSIS	CANADA HEMLOCK	18"-24" SPR.	B-B	
	77	77										TAXUS MEDIA DENSIFORMIS	DENSIFORMIS YEW	18"-24" SPR.	B-B	UNIFORM, FULL
GROUND COVERS	3200	1800		1400								EUONYMUS FORTUNEI COLORATUS	PURPLELEAF WINTERCREEPER	2 YR.	2¼ POTS	MIN. 2 RUNNERS 8"+
	5150	1950	3200									VINCA MINOR	PERIWINKLE, MYRTLE	2 YR.	2¼ POTS	MIN 3-6 RUNNERS 6-8"
VINES	12	12										CELASTRUS SCANDENS	AMERICAN BITTERSWEET	2 YR. NO. 1	1 GAL CONT	MIN. 3 RUNNERS 18"+
	10	10										PARTHENOCISSUS TRICUSPIDATA VEITCHII	VEITCH BOSTON IVY	2 YR. NO. 1	3" POTS	WELL BRANCHED TOP
PERENNIALS	1	1										DICTAMNUS ALBUS	GASPLANT	2 YR. MIN	CONT	HEAVY PLANT, MIN. 5-7 EYES
	2	2										HEMEROCALLIS 'BONANZA'	BONANZA DAYLILY	2 YR. MIN	CONT	HEAVY CLUMPS
	1	1										HEMEROCALLIS 'HYPERION'	HYPERION DAYLILY	2 YR. MIN	CONT	HEAVY CLUMP
	3	3										HOSTA FORTUNEI ALBOMARGINATA	WHITE EDGED PLANTAIN-LILY	2 YR. MIN	CONT	HEAVY CLUMPS
	6	6										HOSTA PLANTAGINEA	FRAGRANT PLANTAIN-LILY	2 YR. MIN	CONT	HEAVY CLUMPS
	800	800										CROCUS VARS.	SPRING FLOWERING CROCUS	TOP SIZE		
	20	20										LILIUM 'ENCHANTMENT'	ENCHANTMENT LILY	TOP SIZE		
	500	500										SCILLA SIBERICA	SIBERIAN SQUILL			

Revisions	Date
6/72 REVIEW	6-22-81

VA FORM 08-6231A, OCT 1978

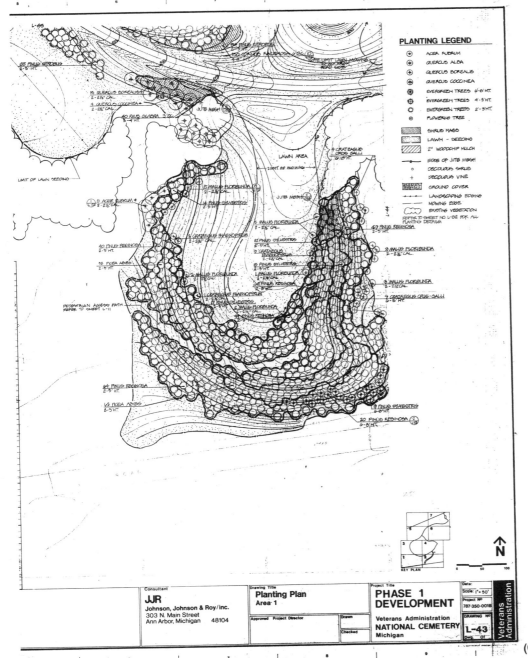

Figure A5-3.

(Courtesy of Johnson, Johnson & Roy, Inc.)

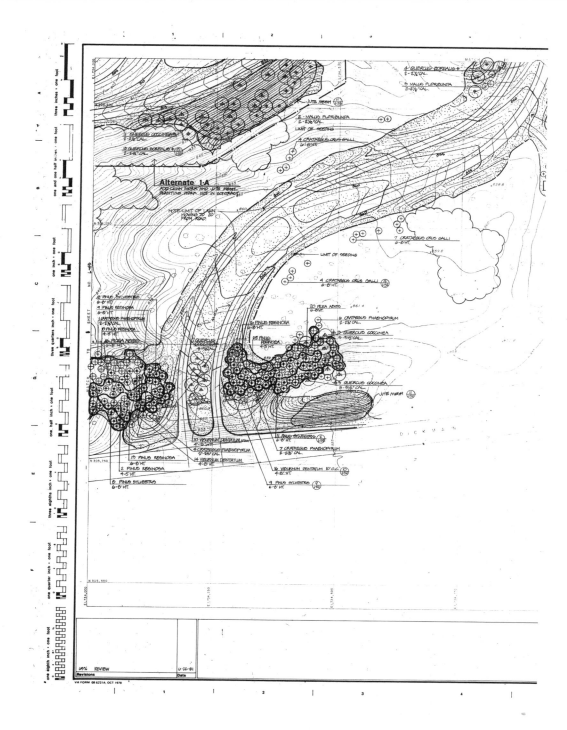

Alternate 1-A

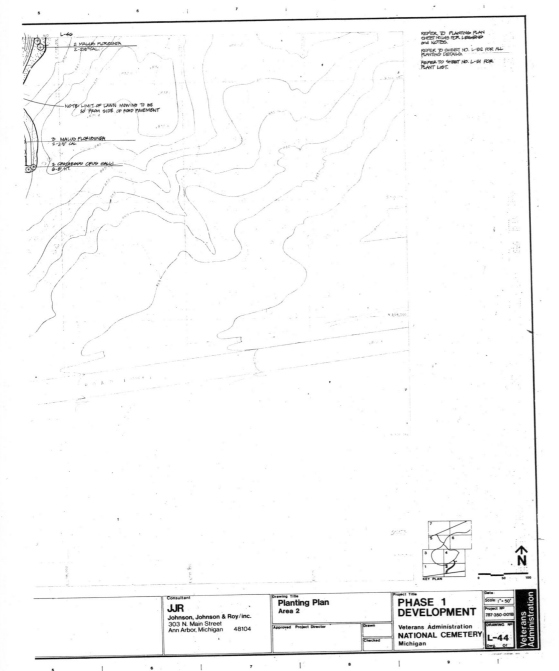

Figure A5-4.
(Courtesy of Johnson, Johnson & Roy, Inc.)

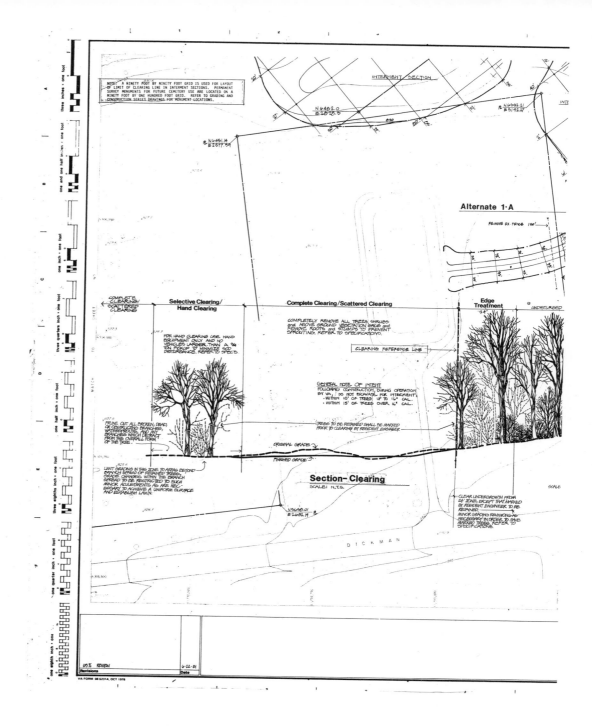

Alternate 1·A

Selective Clearing/
Hand Clearing

Complete Clearing/Scattered Clearing

Edge
Treatment

Section- Clearing
SCALE: N.T.S.

104

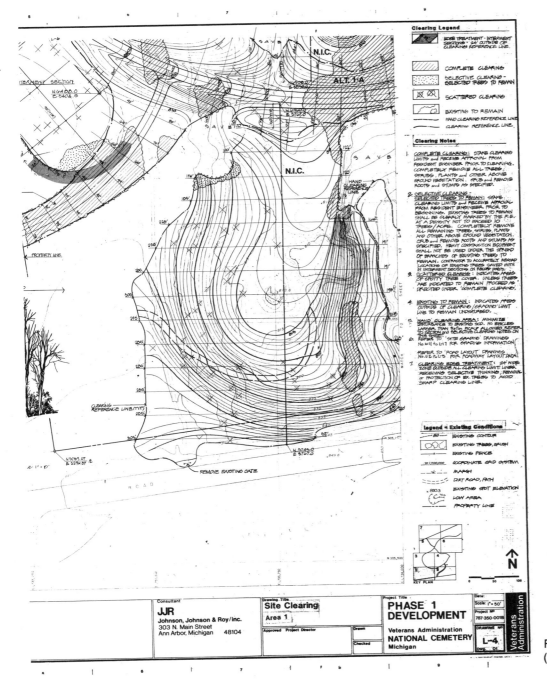

Figure A5–5.
(Courtesy of Johnson, Johnson & Roy, Inc.)

a. *Natural Areas.* In an effort to reduce the amount of energy and maintenance required for lawn mowing, lawn care, etc., it is suggested that certain areas be left to "naturalize" themselves. This would require little or no maintenance. These are areas in which natural grasses and wildflowers could be established. An area where this method could be encouraged is the natural ravine/drainageway north and west of Wengatz Residence Hall, all the way south to Taylor Lake. Other possible areas could be the wooded portions of campus, around Taylor Lake, areas where no outdoor functions take place, etc. (Fig. A5-6).

b. *Open Spaces.* It has been said, "Landscape architecture is to exterior space as architecture is to interior space." Therefore, open spaces are a necessity to the landscape connecting the visual "experiences" with different spatial values. Open spaces form the transitions between various land uses.

2. *Energy Conservation Items.* In addition to the recommendations outlined by the Energy Audit, other considerations for energy conservation might include:

a. Proper location of landscape plantings to maximize solar and wind, etc., control. For example, pine trees should be placed on the north/northwest sides of the buildings to reduce the amount and direction of cold winter winds. Deciduous tree plantings are suggested on the south and west sides of the buildings for summer shade and winter sun. Also, vines growing on building facades provide an insulating value (Fig. A5-7).

b. Passive solar energy should be considered as an energy conservation measure, with the proper positioning of new buildings to achieve maximum solar exposure. All new and future buildings should have southern orientation for this solar benefit.

NATURAL LANDSCAPE

WELL TENDED LAWN

Figure A5-6.
(Courtesy of LeRoy Troyer and Associates)

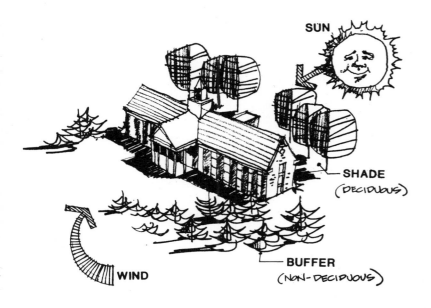

SUN

SHADE
(DECIDUOUS)

BUFFER
(NON-DECIDUOUS)

WIND

Deciduous on South
No-Ndeciduous on North

Figure A5-7. (Courtesy of LeRoy Troyer and Associates)

c. Other energy methods encouraged to be investigated may include:

Use of the earth—"geotexture," an underground air tempering system for heating and cooling.
Use of the wind power.

3. In an effort to strengthen the rural image and define the property of Taylor University, the Master Conceptual Landscape Plan includes development of plantings around the campus edges. This development would include 80- to 120-foot-wide strips in which there are three to four rows of trees/shrubs.... a landscape buffer. On the north and west sides, the outside row of trees is suggested to be an evergreen variety. (This has been started on the west side with the planting of the Colorado Blue Spruces—additional evergreen planting may still be needed.) This would assist in reducing and directing cold winter winds around the campus. The other tree rows should be made up of shade trees and on the inside row, ornamental trees should be planted. The ornamental tree row will serve as an excellent visual foreground, with the larger and darker background being made up of the evergreens and shade trees.

On the south and east sides of the campus property, a similar landscape buffer is suggested, with the exception of the evergreen row. On these property sides, this tree row should be replaced with additional shade trees of a different variety. This will add to the visual environment of the landscape.

The Master Conceptual Landscape Plan suggests that the Campus Tree Nursery be located and be a part of the landscape buffer on the southeast corner of the property. This area could be set up as a nursery and planted with staggered sizes of tree stock at approximately 10 to 12 feet on center. Once the trees reach a transplantable size ($2\frac{1}{2}$ inches diameter), they could be removed and replaced with a small sapling for its growth until harvest. This area could have an ever-changing appearance while the nursery is being used. When the nursery is no longer needed, the trees could then be thinned out to develop as the other landscape buffer strips.

The University should consider the Indiana Department of Natural Resources—Division of Forestry "Tree Farm Program." This program offers an inexpensive source of considerably small sapling plants.

The suggested tree types to be used in these landscape buffer areas are as follows:

Type #1	Type #2	Type #3
Austrian Pine	Sugar Maple	Autumn Olive
White Pine	Red Maple	Washington Hawthorn
Red Pine	Red Oak	Eastern Redbud
Scotch Pine		Flowering Dogwood
Douglas Fir		

The following sketches illustrate these different landscape buffer concepts. (Fig. A5-8)

To reduce the amount of energy needed to mow the large acres of lawn on the Taylor campus, the Landscape Plan suggests areas be developed into what is termed "Natural Landscape." Little maintenance effort will create a natural look, adding to the ground texture surface. Different areas could be planted with prairie grasses, wild flowers, meadow plantings, etc.

After seed is planted, management starts. The objective of management is to increase the competitive advantage that prairie species have over weedy plants. The two key management tools are mowing and burning.

1. The first year, either by hand or by hay mower, mow the growing plants at a height of 6 inches during the third week of June. Again, this will cut the fast early-growing weeds, but will not cut the shorter slower-growing prairie plants.

2. The second year, mow the planting at a height of 6 inches the third week of June. Again, this will cut the early fast-growing weeds but will not cut the shorter slower-growing prairie plants. Other cuttings are recommended if weeds are still dominant or if several prairie species are less than 3 inches high. Remove the clippings if they are thick so they will not kill the small prairie species.

3. Burn the planting the spring of the third year, about the third week of April, if conditions permit. Burning at this time hinders the growth of early-growing weeds and it does little harm to the prairie plants. Burn every second year. Have an experienced burner help the first time or two. Mowing and raking can be substituted when fires are impossible or prohibited.

NOTE: Schedule mowing to meet local growing conditions.

These areas could also be of educational benefit for studying items of succession, etc. In the landscape buffer strips, ground cover material could allow fescue to grow naturally with no need for mowing it.

The landscape plant material used throughout the campus should not only be functional, but also provide maximum seasonal effect. More use of flowering plants that bloom from spring to fall are suggested at important meeting or traffic points throughout the campus. Landscape plantings are also suggested to be of the type and variety to attract wildlife.

Trees should be emphasized in the open areas and trees with shrubs in areas adjacent to buildings and people places. The Conceptual Master Landscape Plan addresses the tree plantings in concept and leaves shrub plantings to be detailed with design and implementation. In the area around the residence halls, it is recommended that various "pockets" of outdoor space be developed into ornamental tree "orchards." The concept would encourage the educational value and stewardship of the land as a part of the students lives. The majestic tree to be used for visual directions on campus malls, etc., is suggested to be Tulip Tree (*Liriodendron tulipifera*), Indiana's state tree.

The following are recommended plant materials for use as trees at Taylor University:

Shade Trees

1.	*Acer platanoides*	Norway Maple
2.	*Acer rubrum*	Red Maple
3.	*Acer saccharum*	Sugar Maple
4.	*Fraxinus americana*	White Ash
5.	*Gleditsia triacanthos*	Honey locust
6.	*Liquidambar styraciflua*	Sweet gum
7.	*Platanus occidentalis*	Sycamore (natural areas only)
8.	*Quercus borealis*	Red Oak

Evergreen Trees

1.	*Picea abies*	Norway Spruce
2.	*Pinus nigra*	Austrian Pine
3.	*Pinus resinosa*	Red Pine
4.	*Pinus sylvestris*	Scotch Pine
5.	*Pseudotsuga menziesii (taxifolia)*	Douglas Fir

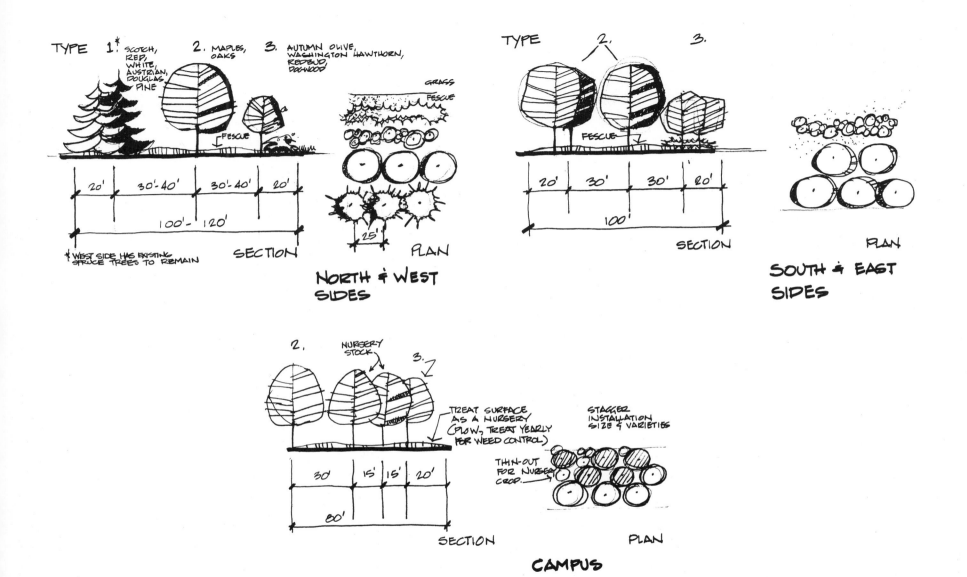

TYPE 1.* SCOTCH, RED, WHITE, AUSTRIAN, DOUGLAS PINE   2. MAPLES, OAKS   3. AUTUMN OLIVE, WASHINGTON HAWTHORN, REDBUD, DOGWOOD

GRASS
FESCUE
FESCUE

20' 30'-40' 30'-40' 20'
100' - 120'

SECTION

PLAN

25'

* WEST SIDE HAS EXISTING SPRUCE TREES TO REMAIN

NORTH & WEST SIDES

TYPE 2. 3.

FESCUE

20' 30' 30' 20'
100'

SECTION

PLAN

SOUTH & EAST SIDES

2. NURSERY STOCK 3.

TREAT SURFACE AS A NURSERY (PLOW, TREAT YEARLY FOR WEED CONTROL)

STAGGER INSTALLATION SIZE & VARIETIES

THIN-OUT FOR NURSERY CROP

30' 15' 15' 20'
80'

SECTION

PLAN

CAMPUS NURSERY PLOT

Figure A5-8. (Courtesy of LeRoy Troyer and Associates)

Ornamental Trees

1. *Cercis canadensis* — Eastern Redbud
*2. *Cornus florida* — Flowering Dogwood
3. *Crataegus phaenopyrum* — Washington Hawthorn
4. *Elaeagnusumbellata* — Autumn Olive
5. *Malus—varieties* — Crabapple Varieties
6. *Pyrus calleryana* — Callery Pear

* Care may be needed for this plant due to existing soil conditions.

Besides the purchased plant material, there exists much plant material on the University's property that could possibly be transplanted to the campus area.

The following (Fig. A5-9) is the Conceptual Master Landscape Plan recommended for implementation by phases. Besides the use of the campus tree nursery, other economic ways for implementing this plan might be by means of civic gifts. After a plan is prepared, various classes may wish to donate either money or labor toward the development of certain sections of the plan in honor of their class.

Regarding the priorities of the Landscape Plan, the following is a recommended list. (These items depend on the development process of other items.)

1. Establish the campus tree nursery.
2. Relocate existing plant material to more appropriate locations due to Master Landscape Plan.
3. Street tree establishment.
4. "Natural Landscape" establishment.

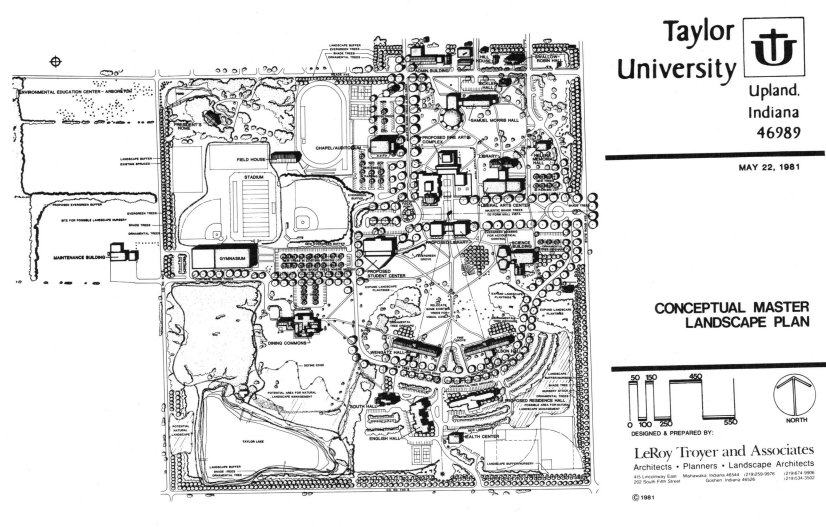

Figure A5-9. (Courtesy of LeRoy Troyer and Associates)

Glossary

adjacent vegetation—the existing or proposed vegetation adjacent to a project site that may influence the planting design of the natural landscape.

aesthetics—the quality of attractiveness or beauty of the natural landscape.

annual—a plant that grows to maturity in one season.

balled and burlapped (B & B)—desired amount of soil still clinging to the roots, roughly in the shape of a ball.

bare-root plants—plants dug out of the soil with little or no soil adhering to them.

barrier—a plant mass used as a partial enclosure of a space or to control pedestrian circulation.

baffle—a plant mass used to control the visual experiences in the natural landscape.

biological components—the plants and animal life of the natural landscape.

blending—the mixing of various vegetative species during the planting process.

caliper—diameter of a tree measured 6 inches (15.24cm) above the ground if up to a 4 inch caliper. For a larger caliper, measurement is made 12 inches (30.48cm) above the ground line.

canopy layer—the highest layer of plants in the natural life forms.

carrying capacity—the number of vegetative types per unit of project area that can be accommodated for any specific period of time, so that the natural characteristics of the species and the quality of the designed environment are sustained indefinitely.

climate—the amount of moisture, wind, and light in the atmosphere of the natural landscape.

climax species—the characteristic species denoting the climax stage of plant growth for a vegetative community.

climax stage—the end result of the vegetative community development process.

critical areas map—the initial planting plan that identifies the most immediate vegetative installations, or the critical planting areas.

critical planting areas—those portions of the site that must be planted to repair surface and subsurface damage.

critical vegetation—the plant materials installed on the critical areas of a site to restore damaged conditions.

cultural components—the past and present land use, existing facilities, aesthetics, and historical attributes of the natural landscape.

deciduous—the term applied to plants that shed their leaves each autumn.

design mix—a mixture of vegetative species blended together for a specific design function.

dibble—a planting bar or instrument used to plant seedling trees.

dormant—temporarily inactive though alive.

ecological niche—particular location suited to a vegetative community.

ecology—the relationship of living things to their environment.

effective depth—the area of soil that is either occupied or has the capability of being occupied by the plant material selected for a design project.

erosion—deterioration brought about by the abrasive action of fluids or solids in motion.

fertilizer—any natural or manufactured material added to the soil in order to supply one or more plant nutrients.

full—a well-branched or well-foliaged plant.

geographic distribution—the geographic area of a plant community.

germination—initial growth or sprouting of a plant.

growing season—any season during which a plant is in growth.

habitat—an environment or locale inhabited by living organisms.

hardy plants—those able to withstand weather conditions without special protection.

host plant—plant associated with, or supporting, insects or diseases.

human impact—the possible harm or damage to a natural landscape by human use.

incline—sloping surface, i.e., neither horizontal nor vertical.

inorganic—substances occurring as minerals in nature or obtainable from them by chemical means.

invader species—the vegetation comprising the initial stages of the successional process.

management capacity—the maximum sustainable level of human use that can be exerted indefinitely without impairment of the natural vegetative systems.

map—a graphic depiction of the surface drawn to scale.

microclimate—the climate of a limited environs.

over-mix—the mixing or blending of various plant species for a design effect.

perennial—plants that live without end as long as the environment is favorable.

permanent vegetation—the material planted on a natural landscape site following the critical vegetation program.

permeability—that property of a porous material that permits the passage of water vapor.

phased plan—the second phase of the planting plan document, following the critical planting plan.

planting bar—see dibble.

reestablishment—the reintroduction of plants into a natural landscape.

resource capacity—the maximum level of use that can be exerted indefinitely on the natural plant components of the resource base without changing the characteristics of the vegetation.

seedbed—the area of the site to which seed is applied.

seed dormancy—the period of time a seed must rest before germination.

site capacity—the number of vegetative types per unit of project area that can be accommodated for any specific period of time, so that the natural characteristics of the species and the quality of the designed environment are sustained indefinitely.

site components—the location, geology, soils, hydrology, and climate of the natural landscape.

soil fertility—the ability of a soil to supply nutrients in sufficient quantity to meet the growth requirements of plants.

sprig—stem fragment used to propagate grasses vegetatively.

succession—progressive replacement of organisms in an ecological sequence until the "climax" material is attained.

terminal—growing end of a branch or stem.

thatch—accumulation of a layer of dead and dying plants.

transpiration—the loss of water vapor from the leaves and stems of living plants.

tuber—short, fleshy, usually underground stem or shoot.

INDEX